P9-DGU-462

CHRISTIANITY RIGHTLY SO CALLED

CHRISTIANITY RIGHTLY SO CALLED

By

SAMUEL G. CRAIG

THE PRESBYTERIAN AND REFORMED PUBLISHING COMPANY

PHILADELPHIA

1957

Distributed
by
BAKER BOOK HOUSE
Grand Rapids 6, Michigan

FIRST PRINTING, APRIL, 1946
SECOND PRINTING, FEBRUARY, 1947
THIRD (REVISED) PRINTING, OCTOBER, 1953
FOURTH (REVISED) PRINTING, 1957

LIBRARY OF CONGRESS CATALOG CARD NUMBER 53-12399

PRINTED IN THE UNITED STATES OF AMERICA

FOREWORD

The aim of this book is to distinguish between Christianity and its counterfeits in a manner understandable by the man in the pew as well as the man in the pulpit. Its purpose is exposition, not defense, and exposition only in as far as needed to make clear what Christianity rightly so called is in distinction from what is wrongly so called. While I have tried to write objectively I have made no attempt to represent myself as neutral in the conflict for and against Christianity as I understand it.

This book is a fruit of my experience as an editor for some twenty-five years—first as editor of *The Presbyterian* and later of *Christianity Today*. It has fallen to my lot during this period not only to peruse many periodicals but to read and review many books, most of them professedly Christian. As a result I have become more and more convinced that nothing is doing more to make matters confused and confusing in the field of religious discussion than the fact that those engaging in it have radically different conceptions of what Christianity is. Men of equal honesty and ability, it may be, come to no agreement because they argue with different conceptions of Christianity in mind. This book is an attempt, however inadequate, to do something to remedy the situation. It seeks to show that whatever may be thought of the truth or value of Christianity there is no good reason why men should be in doubt as to what its essential features are. It is for the reader to judge how successful I have been in my effort.

Among men in general, my sympathies are with all forms of Christianity as over against everything that is other than Christianity. I am primarily interested in the question, What is Christianity? rather than in the question, What is a Christian? However, as will be evident from the chapter entitled "Objective and Sub-Christianity," I am by no means unconcerned about the latter question. Nonetheless the answer to this second question hinges on the answer we give to the first. I am by no means optimistic as regards the number of real Christians there are in the world today. Unquestionably, in my opinion, we are living in the midst of widespread apostasy. Hence either the premillennialists are right in holding that the only hope of the world is in the personal return of Christ to establish His kingdom in this world or repudiating the deformations and falsifications of Christianity which are evident on every side, the Church of Christ must undergo a mighty revival of true religion. Be that as it may, the immediate future is far from bright.

I am a Fundamentalist in the sense that I believe that Christianity has a specific content of its own—factual, doctrinal and ethical—that was given it once and for all by Christ and His Apostles and that only as this content is retained, at least in substance, do we have what can rightly be called Christianity. I have the happiness to know, however, that in this I am in agreement with the members of all the large organized Churches of Christendom—Greek and Roman Catholics as well as Lutheran, Reformed and Wesleyan Protestants—in as far as they are loyal to the doctrinal standards of their Churches. They are all Fundamentalists in this broad sense. It is in this sense, and this sense alone, that I am a Fundamentalist.

The core of this book will be found in the chapter entitled, "The Essential Content of Christianity." What precedes is largely of an introductory nature and what follows is largely an elaboration of its representations and implications in view of opposing conceptions. The discussion is admittedly incomplete inasmuch as there is no discussion of "Christianity and the Church." While I do not share the view of those who look upon the Church as a continuation of the Incarnation I am by no means insensible to its importance. The New Testament knows nothing of isolated Christians. They are all members of the Church. In the classic words of Calvin "the Church is the mother of all those who have God as their Father."

No special claim to originality is made in behalf of this book. Others have labored and I have entered into their labors. The most that can be said is that after gathering material from many sources I have written a book of my own design. On occasion I have quoted from others. In some instances I have done this in the interest of authoritative exposition, in others because of the scholarly reputations of their authors, in still others because their authors have given better expression to what I wanted to say than I had reason to think I could express it myself. Those who share the views of the author will be glad to learn that this book has recently been translated into both Korean and Chinese.

The manuscript of this book was read, in whole or in part, by five friends of various ages. All are university trained, three of them being scholars of wide repute. Only two of them belong to the clergy. Whatever the book's defects they would have been more numerous apart from their criticisms and suggestions.

S. G. C.

March, 1957
Princeton, New Jersey

CONTENTS

CHRISTIANITY RIGHTLY SO CALLED

"And this I pray, that your love may abound yet more in knowledgment and discernment; so that He may distinguish the things that differ."—PHIL. 1:9-10.
(Margin of American Revised Version.)

Chapter I

DEFINITIONS OF CHRISTIANITY

It may seem strange that at this late date, nigh two thousand years after the origin of Christianity, men should be debating the question, What is Christianity? Be that as it may, such is the case. What is more, even among those calling themselves Christians, widely divergent answers are being given and passionately defended. If these answers differed only as regards details, that would merely be what might be expected in view of the fact that even the most erudite of men know only in part. They differ, however, not merely as varieties but rather as species or even genera differ. It is not too much to say that if any of them are measurably true, others of them are largely false. Naturally this is highly confusing to the generality of men.

It should not be supposed that our generation is the first to have differed as regards the right answer to the question, What is Christianity? Such is far from being the case. Of all the generations which have come and gone since Christianity became a factor in this world's affairs there has not been one in which there has not been much difference of opinion as to the correct answer to this question. This was true even in the Middle Ages, the period in which there was the greatest uniformity of opinion relative to the nature and truth of Christianity. What is Christianity? has always been and will ever continue to be the primary question whenever and wherever Christianity is seriously discussed. Such questions as, Is Christianity true? What is the value of Christianity? What are its claims on our acceptance as a way of thought and life? are empty meaningless questions unless and until we know something of what Christianity is. Christianity may be true or it may be false. We are not even in a position to express an opinion as long as we are ignorant of what it is. Christianity may be worthless, even harmful, or it may have a value compared with which the rest of earth's treasures are little more than rubbish. None the less, we cannot appraise it even tentatively as long as we are in the dark as to what it is. Christianity may rightly claim our allegiance both as a system of thought and as a way of life, or it may be the extreme of folly to endeavor to bring our thoughts and activities into harmony with its demands. But certainly we are not qualified to pass judgment on the validity of these claims unless we have a certain amount of knowledge of what it is. This was the primary question at issue between Paul and the Judaizers in the first century, between Irenaeus and the Gnostics in the second century, between Athanasius and Arius in the fourth century, between Augustine and Pelagius in the fifth century, between the Reformers and the Romanists in the sixteenth century, between the Evangelicals and the Deists in the eighteenth century, just as it is the primary question at issue today between the Conservatives and the Liberals or Modernists.

Our generation in debating this question is merely doing what every active, thinking generation for the past nineteen hundred years has been doing and what similar generations that may follow us will do. But while our generation does not differ in kind in this respect from the generations that have preceded us, it does differ much in degree. It surpasses previous generations both in the number and diversity of the things called Christianity, and the extent to which they are at variance with each other.

The Riot of Definitions

The number and diversity of the things called Christianity are truly amazing. Their number and diversity are such that it is even questionable whether the word "Christianity," as currently used, has any definite meaning. At any rate, so different are the meanings attached to it today that it may, not without warrant, be compared to a jar or bottle into which men may pour whatever content their convenience may dictate. Some mean by Christianity, the redemptive supernaturalism of the Bible. Others identify it with morality or, more narrowly, with morality of a Christ-like sort. Still others identify it with altruism or the sentiment of loyalty to the community. Closely related to those just mentioned are those who identify it with sacrificial good will creative of fellowship or brotherhood. Some commend a Christianity without miracles; others tell us that a Christianity without miracles is just no Christianity at all. Some commend a non-doctrinal Christianity; others tell us that, since Christianity is an historical religion and its doctrines the interpretation of the facts that lie at its basis, a non-doctrinal Christianity is inconceivable. Some commend a Christless Christianity or at least a Christianity to which Christ himself is not indispensable; others tell us that Christianity and Christ are one to such a degree that to speak of a Christless Christianity is to be guilty of a contradiction in terms—that one with equal warrant could speak of wooden iron or a square circle. Some even commend an atheistic Christianity. This is not altogether surprising. It is quite compatible with those definitions of Christianity which identify it with altruism, brotherhood, sacrificial good will and such like. If we were attempting to enumerate all the things called Christianity today we would have to make mention of Mormonism, Christian Science, Theosophy, Russellism, Spiritualism, New Thought—and what not? It goes without saying that the number and diversity of the things called Christianity today are very confusing, so confusing that many will think that W. R. Matthews put it mildly when in his Boyle Lectures, having in mind that impression of "incoherent diversity" which the ordinary man can hardly fail to receive from hearing such a multitude of things called Christianity, he said: "I can imagine a man exclaiming, in no flippant spirit, that it is more difficult to discover what Christianity is than to believe it when it be discovered." [1]

Yesterday and Today

It is when we consider the diversity of things called Christianity today that we perceive the difference between the existing situation and the situation in previous ages—with the possible exception of the first three centuries when Christianity was engaged in a life and death struggle with the heathen religions of Greece and Rome. In former generations the issue was, for the most part at least, between more or less adequate and more or less inadequate answers to the question, What is Christianity? At the present time, the issue is in large part between answers which involve the very right of Christianity as understood by men of former days, despite their differences, to exist at all. This is true to such a degree that the heirs of the Reformers, though as unflinchingly opposed to Rome as were their fathers, today see in Roman Catholicism an ally as over against a common enemy, an enemy that in their judgment retains nothing distinctive of Christianity but the name. The reason for this appears as soon as we perceive where the main battle lines are drawn today. "A so-called orthodox Protestant," said Dr. Abraham Kuyper in words that are as true today as when he uttered them at the turn of the century, "need only mark on his confession and catechism such doctrines of religion and morals as are not subject

[1] *Studies in Christian Philosophy,* p. 36.

to controversy between Rome and ourselves to perceive immediately that what we have in common with Rome concerns precisely those fundamentals of our Christian creed now most fiercely assaulted by the modern spirit—Theism over against Atheism and Pantheism; sin over against imperfection; the divine Christ of God over against Jesus the mere man; the cross a sacrifice of reconciliation over against the cross as a symbol of martyrdom; the Bible as given by inspiration of God over against a purely human product; the Ten Commandments as ordained of God over against a mere archaeological document; the ordinances of God absolutely established over against an ever-changing law and morality spun out of man's subjective consciousness. Now, in this conflict, Rome is not an antagonist, but stands at our side; inasmuch as she also recognizes and maintains the Trinity, the deity of Christ, the Cross as an atoning sacrifice, the Scriptures as the Word of God, and the Ten Commandments as a divinely imposed rule of life." [2]

What has been said of the differences between Protestants and Roman Catholics may be said with far more warrant of the differences between Calvinists and Lutherans or between Calvinists and Arminians. However great the differences between Protestants and Protestants or even between Protestants and Roman Catholics they are relatively small as compared with the difference between all of them and many calling themselves Christians

[2] *Lectures on Calvinism* (Wm. B. Eerdmans Pub Co.), pp. 275-276.

today—a difference so radical that the universal acceptance of their religious conceptions would mean that Christianity, as traditionally understood, had become a dead religion. As truly as in the first three centuries, Christianity as it has been generally understood is engaged in a life and death struggle for its very existence. It is being attacked all along the line. It is no longer subject to merely flank attacks—attacks which, if they had proved successful, would have exposed its main line of defense to possible destruction. It is being attacked on the front as well as from all sides by those who demand its unconditional surrender and who would fain leave it without name or remainder on the earth.

The Rise and Spread of the Naturalistic World and Life View

That Christianity faces a more serious situation today than in any previous period, with the possible exception of the first three centuries, finds its explanation in the rise and spread of the empirico-scientific world and life view that made its appearance in the so-called Enlightenment of the eighteenth century, later clarified, strengthened and extended under the influence of Hume, Kant, Darwin and others. Previous to that time the various world and life views that had prevailed, no matter when or where, had been supernaturalistic to the core. Nothing, however, is more characteristic of the empirico-scientific view than its thoroughgoing naturalism—the resoluteness with which it seeks to explain the entire world, including man and religion and morality, without the aid of any supernatural factor, purely from resident forces and according to unvarying laws. In the nature of the case, it thereby assumed a position of determined and thorough-going opposition to Christianity such as had characterized no previous world and life view. And that because, as we trust will be made clear in later chapters, the supernatural is to such an extent the animating principle of Christianity that Christianity de-supernaturalized is Christianity extinct. While we must go back more than two hundred years to discover the roots of this purely naturalistic world and life view, it is only within the last hundred years that it has gained acceptance sufficiently wide to awaken within its devotees the courage to launch an all-out attack upon Christianity. At first its advocates rejected only the doctrines of Christianity together with the supernatural facts of which the doctrines are the explanation but continued to extol the superiority of the Christian ethic. It is not more than seventy-five years since John Stuart Mill declared that it "would not be easy, even for the unbeliever, to find a better translation of the rule of virtue from the abstract to the concrete than to endeavor so to live that Christ would approve our life" [3]—a declaration that reflected what was then and what for some time thereafter was the common view even among those who rejected the supernaturalism of preceding ages, including that

[3] *Three Essays in Religion,* p. 253.

of Christianity. This was the view, for instance, of Thomas Huxley, Matthew Arnold, George Eliot, Mrs. Humphrey Ward and other influential writers. Today, however, the situation has reached such a stage that no part of Christianity is more openly assailed than its ethics. Nietzsche was the first influential thinker openly to attack the Christian ideal of conduct. So significant did he consider this attack that he counted it as his chief claim to distinction that he had exposed the real nature of the Christian ethic. "That which deifies me, that makes me stand apart from the whole of the rest of mankind," he wrote in *Ecce Homo,* "is the fact that I have unmasked Christian morality. Christian morality is the most malignant form of all falsehood, the actual Circe of humanity, that which has corrupted mankind." [4] H. G. Wells, Bertrand Russell, Bernard Shaw, Freud and others may be more restrained in their mode of expression, but they are wholly one with Nietzsche in their repudiation of Christian standards of conduct and in holding that the man most to be admired is other than the Christian man. It may be true that the great majority of naturalists still deny that in repudiating the supernatural they are undermining Christian morality, but this majority is rapidly diminishing and it is coming more and more to be recognized that the revolt against the Christian ethic, so widely prevalent today, is due to a previous repudiation of the doctrines upon which it is founded—doctrines which, as we shall

[4] p. 139.

endeavor to make clear later, are indissolubly bound up with the supernatural.

Having directed attention to the rise and spread of the empirico-scientific world and life view which has so profoundly affected the thinking of our age and generation, we are better prepared to classify the various definitions of Christianity that are being commended for our acceptance. The line of cleavage between these definitions is by no means clear. They are often expressed in such a vague way or overlap to such an extent that it is difficult if not impossible to indicate precisely wherein they differ. For the most part, however, they can be assigned to two main classes—the supernatural and the anti-supernatural. Whatever may have been true in previous ages, it is hardly open to denial that the clearest and deepest line of cleavage between those calling themselves Christians today is between those who are basically supernaturalistic and those who are basically naturalistic in their conception of Christianity.

The Supernaturalists

Most of those calling themselves Christians are supernaturalists of the traditional type, *i.e.*, they hold to the high supernaturalism of the Biblical writers—a supernaturalism that includes the supernatural in the form of the miraculous.

The fact that the anti-supernaturalists are more vocal should not be allowed to conceal the fact that the overwhelming majority of those calling themselves Christians still hold to the high supernaturalism that was dominant in Christian circles until the rise and spread of the modern world view of which we have just made mention. While the space devoted to supernaturalism in *American Philosophies of Religion* by Henry Nelson Wieman and Bernard Eugene Meland (15 out of 348 pages) is fitted to suggest that there are relatively few supernaturalists today and while its authors assert that "its strength is waning" yet they not only admit that "the majority of religious people in the United States still follow the way of traditional supernaturalism" but that "it is stronger than any of its competitors" and that "none of these as yet show signs of inheriting its power." [5] The most significant fact to be taken into consideration in this connection is that the creeds of the entire organized Church—Orthodox Greek, Roman Catholic and Protestant—bear consentient witness to a Christianity that is through and through supernaturalistic. However much naturalistic views have seeped into the minds of the members of these Churches—and undoubtedly they have done so to a large extent especially in certain branches of the Protestant churches—it can hardly be denied that to the vast majority of those who call themselves Christians the supernatural enters into the substance of what they regard as Christianity to such a degree that they would not hesitate to say that Christianity shorn of the supernatural is Christianity falsely so called. They believe in God as a supernatural fact, in miracles as supernatural acts of that supernatural God, in redemption as

[5] pp. 62 and 65.

the work of a supernatural Christ, in the Christian life as due to the supernatural work of a supernatural Spirit, and in an immortality that cannot be expressed in naturalistic terms. While it may not be altogether surprising that many of the anti-supernaturalists, in view of the gains they have registered within the last fifty years, are looking upon supernatural Christianity as an out-moded position and looking forward with confidence to the day when this shall be everywhere perceived, they must perforce admit that as yet they are a small minority among those who profess and call themselves Christians. Professedly non-Christians, in the nature of the case, do not count in this connection.

The Naturalists

There was a time, not at all remote, when to speak of a purely naturalistic Christianity would have been regarded as a contradiction in terms. That was, however, before the rise of the anti-supernaturalistic world and life view in the eighteenth century and the attempts which have been made within the last one hundred years so to modify, transform or refashion the Christianity of the past so as to bring it into harmony with naturalistic science and naturalistic criticism. Today, however, matters have reached a stage in which many of the answers being given to the question, What is Christianity?, in the books and magazines pouring from our presses are naturalistic in character. Some of these answers are naturalistic in the sense of being materialistic or pantheistic, and so for all practical purposes atheistic in character, but most of them are theistic in character and naturalistic only in the sense that they allow for no intrusion of the supernatural in the course of this world's development, *i.e.,* they do not allow for the supernatural in the form of the miraculous. Whatever we may think of a non-miraculous Christianity, we can hardly fail to be impressed by the zeal of its advocates. They are so vocal that the uninformed are apt to get the impression that they outnumber the advocates of traditional Christianity.

Anti-supernaturalists may be sub-divided into Liberals and Modernists for, while both are basically naturalistic in their thinking, they employ different methods to explain the fact—admitted by all—that, until rather recently, nearly all of those calling themselves Christians were out-and-out supernaturalists.

In using the words "Liberal" and "Modernist" to designate the different methods employed to explain Christianity without having recourse to the supernatural, we are aware that these words are often used interchangeably and so without any real difference of meaning. It seems to us, however, that it is not without warrant that some use the words discriminately—the former to designate those who have followed in the footsteps of Adolf Harnack and the latter those who have followed rather the example of Alfred Loisy. Harnack, it will be recalled, having derived from the Gospels (as reconstructed by him according to his naturalistic presuppositions) his conception of the Christianity of Jesus, saw in this primitive Christianity (so-called) the standard of all subsequent Christianity and so maintained that nothing belonged to its essence that was not to be found in those primitive beginnings. Loisy, however, saw in the Christianity of Jesus only the germ from which Christianity as he understood it had grown. He found Christianity not in its germ but in its full growth. For him, the main thing is not what Christianity was in its beginnings, but what it is like today and what it is on the way of becoming tomorrow.

The Liberals

According to the Liberals, as we have defined them, almost the entire historical manifestation of Christianity represents a radical departure from type. They hold that almost immediately after the death of Christ the "religion of Jesus," which they think was naturalistic, was transformed, refashioned, made over, radically altered, under the influence of the pre-Christian beliefs of His earliest followers. The religion of the "primitive community" was in turn overlaid and transformed by the theological constructions of Paul, with the result that it is Paulinism rather than Christianity with which church history for the most part concerns itself. These scholars all but unanimously admit that the Christianity which has dominated the ages is essentially one with Paulinism. This means that, since Paul, Christianity has adhered rather closely to type. However, they maintain that there are two high mountains through which we must tunnel, as it were, if we are to get back of Paulinism to the religion of Jesus. The first lies between Paulinism and the religion of the "primitive community"; the second, between the religion of the "primitive community" and the "religion of Jesus." Wrede, with the first in mind, says that it was Paul who "introduced into Christianity the ideas whose influence on its history up to the present time has been the deepest and most far-reaching." [6] Henry C. Vedder, with both in mind, declared that "the publication of the words of Jesus in the Gospels found men's minds preoccupied with other ideas, and his teaching made little impression. The Christians of A.D. 80, and afterwards, supposed they were following closely in the footsteps of the Master, when they had really cast aside the most important of his instructions and adopted an ideal of life altogether foreign to his. It required nineteen centuries after that for men to catch sight once more of what Jesus intended and hoped to accomplish." [7]

The classic expression of the Liberal conception of Christianity is still to be found in Harnack's *What is Christianity?* According to Harnack the teaching of Jesus can, as a whole, be subsumed under three heads: "the kingdom of God and its coming," "God and the infinite value of the human soul," and "the higher righteousness and the commandment of love." He affirmed that

[6] *Paul*, p. 179.

[7] *The Fundamentals of Christianity* (The Macmillan Co.), p. 97.

"Christ's message appears in the clearest and most direct light when grasped in connection with the idea of God the Father and the infinite value of the human society" and that this "shows that the Gospel is in no wise a positive religion like the rest, that it contains no statutory or particularistic element, that it is therefore religion itself."[8] It is especially significant to note that Harnack affirmed that "the Gospel as Jesus proclaimed it has to do with the Father only and not with the Son," as this necessarily means that Jesus did not occupy an essential place in the religion He taught. The bulk of Liberals still walk in Harnack's footsteps inasmuch as they define Christianity in such a way that the position which Jesus occupies in it is that of a pioneer teacher and example, *i.e.*, as occupying in Christianity a position similar to that which Luther occupies in Lutheranism or Calvin in Calvinism. Jesus is deemed valuable, but His value lies in the moral and religious ideals He taught and exemplified rather than in His person. Some of the more radical of the Liberals do not hesitate to say that their moral and religious lives would not suffer shipwreck, even if it should be discovered that Jesus never lived. Liberals find the essence of Christianity in altruism, Christlikeness, sacrificial good will, loyalty to the community, brotherhood and such like—traits of character and modes of activity that may exist, in some degree at least, even where Christ is unknown or ignored.

[8] p. 63.

The Modernists

Modernists, as we have defined these, both Catholic and Protestant, hold with the Liberals that Christianity has not conformed to type. Their critical attitude toward the New Testament literature is very similar to that of the Liberals. However, when they have recovered the "Christianity of Christ," they do not identify it with true Christianity and use it as a norm to distinguish between its originally pure and its late corrupt manifestations, as do the Liberals, but merely see in it the seed out of which the tree of Christianity, as we know it, has grown. If the Liberals show a tendency to treat the historical development of Christianity as though it had no bearing on the question, What is Christianity?, the Modernists, on the contrary, show a tendency to regard its earliest manifestation as seen in Jesus and his more immediate disciples, as relatively unimportant in answering this question. With them, Christianity is a living and growing thing; the important matter is not what it was two thousand years ago but what it is today. There is a sense in which Liberals speak of a "faith once delivered," since they find the essence of Christianity in altruism, Christlikeness and such like—qualities of character which they hold will never be surpassed. It is quite otherwise however with the Modernists. With them the phrase, "once for all delivered," is taboo. With them, the Christianity of the twentieth century is and ought to be quite different from the Christianity of the first century. What meets us in the New Testament, according to them, is in no sense a grown tree whose leaves are for the healing of the nations but rather the seed from which Christianity, as we have it today, has grown. Lyman Abbot was writing under the influence of this point of view—the pioneer and outstanding representative of which was, as we have said, Loisy—when he wrote: "The Christianity of the twentieth century is not the same as the Christianity of Jesus Christ; and it ought not to be. For Christianity is a life, and after nineteen centuries of growth it can no more be the same it was in the first century than an oak is the same as an acorn." [9] Harry Emerson Fosdick under the same influence wrote: "The progressiveness of Christianity is not simply its response to a progressive age; the progressiveness of Christianity springs from its own inherent vitality. So far is this from being regrettable, that a modern Christian rejoices in it and gladly recognizes not only that he is thinking thoughts and undertaking enterprises which his fathers would not have understood, but also that his children after him will differ quite as much in teaching and practice from the modernity of today." [10] George Cross, late of Rochester Seminary, wrote: "It must not be assumed that there are available for our use any fixed standard tests for the final determination of what is truly Christian as distinct from that which claims to be Christian. . . . It is even pos-

[9] *What Christianity Means to Me,* Prologue, p. 7.
[10] *Christianity and Progress* (Fleming H. Revell Co.), p. 164.

sible, and we say it with reverence for him in our hearts, that if all the teachings of Jesus were brought together in the exact form in which he gave them there might be found among them some that would not commend themselves as fixed and final to the most intelligent and devout Christians of the present day. . . . The Christianity of yesterday was creative of the Christianity of today and at the same time the Christianity of today is more and something other than the Christianity of yesterday. For it recreates that which came from the past and makes it over."[11]

The Neo-Supernaturalists

There is a group that must be reckoned with in any present day classification of those calling themselves Christians that do not obviously belong to either of the groups mentioned. At any rate there is considerable difference of opinion as to the extent to which they are basically naturalistic or basically supernaturalistic in their conception of Christianity. We refer to the neo-supernaturalists, often called the neo-orthodox. As the name implies, they are of recent origin as compared with the traditional supernaturalists. They are, in fact, of more recent origin than their name might suggest as they were virtually unheard of, in this country at least, until some time after the First World War. For, while neo-supernaturalism is rooted in the Critical philosophy of Kant, especially as modified by Soren Kierkegaard and Martin Heidegger, it is largely indebted to

11 *Creative Christianity* (The Macmillan Co.), pp. 26, 34 and 52.

Karl Barth and Emil Brunner for its present vogue. Many of the neo-supernaturalists have come from the ranks of those who once held a purely naturalistic conception of Christianity but who, discontented with such a conception, have reverted more or less fully to the supernaturalism of historic Christianity. However, they, as a class, still hold that modern science has rendered untenable the view of nature generally held before the rise of the empirico-scientific world view, and that literary and historical criticism has made it impossible to identify the words of the Bible with the Word of God. Hence, in the nature of the case, they profess only such supernaturalism as may be held in harmony with a more or less naturalistic modern science and with a more or less naturalistic modern criticism of the Bible. It seems clear that some of them are basically naturalistic in their conception of Christianity. Others of them, whether consistently or not, hold to a degree of supernaturalism, usually under the name of the super-historical, which seems to remove them from the naturalists and to put them among the supernaturalists. It is no part of our task to indicate to what extent the neo-supernaturalists are properly classed with the naturalists and to what extent with the supernaturalists but merely to point out that some of those so designated apparently belong to one class and some to the other. In the case of some, the word "neo-supernaturalists" would seem to be a misnomer but, in the case of others, their belief in the super-historical, however difficult it may be to define just what they mean by it, separates them more or less sharply from the naturalists in the field of science while their belief that God speaks to men through the words of the Bible separates them even more sharply from those who maintain that the Bible does not differ in kind from other religious literature. Wrong in our opinion, will be the verdict history will pass on the claim that some of them have arrived or at least show promise of arriving, at a "tenable fundamentalism." [12]

Doctrine of Salvation Involved

The depth and the width of the gulf that divides between the naturalistic and the supernaturalistic conceptions of Christianity is not perceived unless it is perceived that it divides between two conceptions of salvation. We are not merely concerned with the difference between two world views but equally between two life views, more particularly with the difference between two answers to the question, What must I do to be saved? Fundamentally, there are but two doctrines of salvation: the natural, according to which salvation is from ourselves, and the supernatural, according to which salvation is from God. The former assumes that man is to save himself, that he is literally the architect of his own fortunes, the carver of his own destiny. The latter, however, assumes that if man is to be saved at all he must be saved by a power outside of himself, that there

[12] Dr. Cornelius Van Til, author of what is still the most thorough critique of this movement that has yet appeared, is very much of the opinion that this verdict will be unfavorable. See *The New Modernism: An Appraisal of the Theology of Barth and Brunner.*

is no such thing as a self-made Christian, that the highest type of man is one who says with Paul, "By the grace of God I am what I am" (I Cor. 15:10). The naturalists, with one voice, hold to the former because in the nature of the case they are precluded from holding any other view. The supernaturalists not only may but as a class do hold to the latter view, as evidenced by the fact that it is held by the entire organized Christian Church. No doubt, naturalistic views of salvation have pervaded to a considerable extent the membership of the churches but the entire organized Church—Greek Orthodox, Roman Catholic, and Protestant—are at one in professing the supernaturalistic conception of salvation, if we except those of such questionable standing as the Unitarians.

We would not be understood as saying that, previous to the eighteenth century, both these doctrines of salvation were not held by those calling themselves Christians. They were. Witness the Judaizers in the first century and the Pelagians in the fifth. Moreover, what was true in the days of Paul and Augustine has been true in varying degrees during all the years that have followed. Since the rise and spread of the anti-supernaturalistic world and life view, however, the disparity between these two methods of salvation has become increasingly clear. Among those calling themselves Christians today are those who outpelagianize Pelagius in the completeness with which they teach that man is his own saviour. For, while Pelagius taught that Christ had made expiation for past sin, our modern Pelagians will hear nothing whatever of expiation and declare not only that man stands in no need of supernatural help in working out his salvation but that none is available. The difference between the naturalistic and the supernaturalistic views of life and the world has brought into the sharpest possible relief the question whether, according to the Christian scheme of things, man saves himself or whether he is saved by God.

We have sought to indicate the number and diversity of the things called Christianity today for the purpose of making clear the need, the crying need, of distinguishing between the things rightly called Christianity and the things falsely so called. Nothing is doing more to make matters confused and confusing, in the sphere of religious discussion, than the fact that so many of those who engage in it have radically different notions of what Christianity is. Men of equal ability and sincerity, it may be, come to no agreement in discussing the issues before the Church because some argue with one conception of Christianity in mind and some with another. Nothing is more needed today, we are convinced, than a clear understanding of what Christianity is. It may be and doubtless is a high tribute to the reputation Christianity has gained that those who have so little in common as the naturalists and the supernaturalists, who are at loggerheads at every crucial position, should yet strive for a monopoly of the name. As matters stand, it is not necessarily a comfort to a Christian to have another tell him that he also is a Christian because what this other calls Christianity may lack all that is most distinctive of what he calls Christianity. In that case, if what the other calls Christianity is really Christianity what he calls Christianity is not rightly so called. To use the word Christianity to designate radically different things is to employ it as a word without definite content—a word that may be used to express whatever one may happen to believe in the sphere of religion. It may be true that a rose by any other name would smell as sweet. It does not follow, however, that whatever we may call a rose will possess a rose's fragrance. What is Christianity rightly so called? That is the question that will concern us in the chapters that follow.

"That which was from the beginning, which we have heard, which we have seen with our eyes, which we have looked upon, and our hands have handled, of the Word of life (for the life was manifested, and we have seen it, and bear witness, and shew unto you that eternal life, which was with the Father, and was manifested unto us); that which we have seen and heard declare we unto you, that ye may have fellowship with us: and truly our fellowship is with the Father and with His Son Jesus Christ."
—I JOHN 1:1-3.

Chapter II

CHRISTIANITY AND HISTORY

We have indicated the diversity and multiplicity of the answers being given to the question, What is Christianity? What we have written is no doubt fitted to create the impression that the question with which we are concerned is a difficult one. Otherwise why is there such a diversity of answers given and defended by those calling themselves Christians? None the less we do not believe that it requires any special scholarship or any extraordinary ability to discover with substantial accuracy what Christianity really is. The situation is indeed confusing because so many coins, bearing the image and superscription of Christianity, are in circulation; and yet, we believe, that it is easily possible for the plain man, by the use of only such care and discretion as he exercises in his common, everyday life, to distinguish between the genuine and the counterfeit. To show that this is the case is the object of this chapter.

It is often assumed that we can obtain a sufficiently exact answer to the question with which we are concerned by ascertaining what is held in common by those professing and calling themselves Christians—what is held in common being regarded as essential, and what is not as unessential. This is the method advocated, for instance, by Professor Edgar S. Brightman of Boston University. In an article entitled "The Essence of Christianity" and published in the Crozer Quarterly (April, 1941), he concludes his summary of what he regards the essentials of Christianity with the words: "Our attempt has been to define Christianity by seeking for beliefs and attitudes held in common throughout Christian history by all the followers of Jesus."

This method, however, is fatally defective whether we employ it having in mind all those who throughout the Christian centuries have called themselves Christians, or only those who today in different areas of the world call themselves Christians. Suppose that among those who have called themselves Christians in the past or who call themselves Christians today there are those who are not Christians at all either in thought or life. It can scarcely be denied that in all ages, including the present, there have been tares among the wheat, goats among the sheep. Since this is the case, since among those professing and calling themselves Christians there have been and are those who are not Christians, what has been held or is held in common lacks the marks distinctive of Christianity. Hence any answer obtained by this method alone will necessarily be fatally defective. But even if all those who have called or do call themselves Christians were, or are, really Christians, the employment of this method can only give us the minimum of Christianity, the very least that a man can profess in word and deed and still honestly and intelligently call himself a Christian. Otherwise, the more attenuated forms of Christianity of which we have knowledge would be excluded. Suppose we ask the question, What is a man? In putting this question, do we merely want to ascertain what all men have had or have in common? If so, we are inquiring concerning the poorest, meanest, least developed specimen—physically, intellectually, morally and spiritually—that exists or ever has existed that could properly be called a man. Do we not rather want to be told what normal, representative man is? Surely that is what Shakespeare had in mind when he wrote: "What a piece of work is man! How noble in reason! In form and moving how express and admirable! In action how like an angel! In apprehension how like a god! the beauty of the world! the paragon of animals!" [1] Surely also it is not otherwise when we ask, What is Christianity? We are inquiring what normal, representative Christianity is, not what is the most attenuated, contentless thing that can possibly be called Christianity. Even if all called Christians, either by themselves or by others, are really such, this method will only give us the minimum of Christianity, not normal, representative Christianity. But, unless we are wholly wrong in thinking that there has been—and is—much counterfeit Christianity in the world, it will not give us even that. In that case it will give us only what Christianity has in common with natural religion. No doubt Christianity and natural religion have

[1] *Hamlet.* Act II, Scene 2.

much in common; but what they have in common lacks everything that is distinctive of Christianity.

We would not be understood as alleging that this method is wholly useless—there may have been periods of history in which a fairly accurate conception of Christianity could be obtained by merely taking into consideration what Christians confessed in common—but unquestionably its use is limited and, as an exclusive method, it cannot but lead astray. Whatever value it may have had at times, it has little value today in view of the radical difference of opinion among those who profess and call themselves Christians.

Christianity an Historical Entity

We have seen that the notion that we can obtain a substantially correct answer to the question, What is Christianity?, by taking note of what those calling themselves Christians hold in common is fatally defective. It has to its credit, however, that it has some realization of the fact that this question is primarily an historical question. It is the failure to recognize this which is mainly responsible, we are persuaded, for the variety of answers being given to this question. It is hardly too much to say that a proper recognition of this fact is all that is needed to make clear that there is nothing particularly difficult about the question, What is Christianity? At the bottom of most, if not all, of the confusion over what Christianity is, is blindness to the fact that the question, What is Christianity?, is first, last and always an historical question. This being the case, it must be approached as such if it is to be approached intelligently.

The question, What is Christianity?, does not differ in kind from the questions, What is Darwinism? What is Mohammedanism? How do we go about it to learn what Darwinism is? Is it not by reading the writings of Darwin with the help, perhaps, of his representative disciples? And how do we find out what Mohammedanism is? Is it not by reading the Koran with the help, it may be, of its representative expositors? And how otherwise ought we to proceed in endeavoring to ascertain what Christianity is? We may or we may not approve of Darwinism but, at any rate, it is the writings of Darwin that constitute the primary source of information for those who desire to know what it is. Again, we may or may not approve of Mohammedanism but, be our personal attitude toward it what it may, the primary source of learning what it is, is the Koran. And so we may or may not approve of Christianity but, however that may be, we must direct our attention to Christ and His Apostles as our primary source of information if we are to be certain that we know what it really is in distinction from something that is merely called Christianity. What Christianity is, as Dr. J. Gresham Machen has pointed out, is "subject to historical investigation exactly as is the assertion that the Roman Empire under Nero was a free democracy. Possibly the Roman Empire under Nero would have been better if it had been a free democracy, but the historical question is simply whether as a matter of fact it was a free democracy or not. Christianity is an historical phenomenon, like the Roman Empire, or the Kingdom of Prussia, or the United States of America. And as an historical phenomenon it must be investigated on the basis of historical evidence. . . . The question can be settled only by an examination of the beginnings of Christianity. Recognition of this fact does not involve any acceptance of Christian belief; it is merely a matter of common sense and common honesty. At the foundation of the life of every corporation is the incorporation paper, in which the objects of the corporation are set forth. Other objects may be vastly more desirable than those objects, but if the directors use the name and the resources of the corporation to pursue the other objects they are acting *ultra vires* of the corporation. So it is with Christianity. It is perfectly conceivable that the originators of the Christian movement had no right to legislate for subsequent generations; but at any rate they did have an inalienable right to legislate for all generations that should choose to bear the name of 'Christian.' It is conceivable that Christianity may now have to be abandoned, and another religion substituted for it; but at any rate the question what Christianity is can be determined only by an examination of the beginnings of Christianity." [2]

It cannot be too much emphasized, or too often reiterated, that in dealing with the question, What

[2] *Christianity and Liberalism* (Wm. B. Eerdmans Pub. Co.), p. 20.

is Christianity?, we are dealing with an historical question, one whose answer must be sought in the field of history. Such questions as, Is Christianity true? What is the value of Christianity? Is Christianity acceptable to the modern man?, must be held in abeyance, as far as possible, until we have ascertained what it is. Christianity may be as false as some maintain, as lacking in value as others allege or as outmoded as still others assert; but what has that to do with what it is? The multitude of conflicting answers being given to this question finds its explanation, in large part at least, in an initial failure to perceive that it is primarily an historical question. The historical question, What is Christianity?, is all too frequently confused with the rational question, Is it true? or the ethical question, Is it moral? or the practical question, Is it useful? or with the more philosophical question, Does it constitute the ideal religion?

An excellent illustration of what results from treating the question, What is Christianity?, as other than an historical question may be found in an article entitled, "What is the Christian Religion?" by Douglas Clyde Macintosh, late Professor of Theology in Yale Divinity School, and published in the *Harvard Theological Review* (January, 1914). While the article was published some thirty years ago it has lost none of its significance with the passing years especially as there are many today who seem equally blind to the real nature of the question we are considering. In this article Dr. Macintosh asserted that redemption by the blood of Christ as a sacrifice for sin is "not only not essential to Christianity *because contrary to reason,* but moreover essentially unchristian *because opposed to the principles of sound morality.*" He further asserted that the Christian religion "must be in essence whatever in actual Christianity is *necessary for the realization of the true ideal of human spiritual life in general and of human religion in particular*" (italics ours). Dr. Macintosh has given us a glaring instance of dealing with Christianity as other than an historical phenomenon. He characterizes certain ideas as unchristian because they do not harmonize with his conception of what is rational and moral and with what he conceives to be the ideal religion. It may be a matter of interest to know what a professor of theology in one of the leading theological schools of this country regarded as rational or moral or in harmony with ideal religion, but it is difficult to see that this addition to our fund of knowledge has any particular bearing on the question of what Christianity is. No doubt if we find in Christianity that which is really irrational or immoral or unideal we ought, to that extent, to reject it, but that does not justify us in saying that these to us irrational or immoral or unideal elements are not essential elements of Christianity. It is at least conceivable that they are essential to its very existence. Certainly we have no right to assume that such is not the case. Obviously we have no more right to approach the question, What is Christianity?, with the assumption that it is the ideal religion and as such thoroughly rational and moral than we have to approach the question, What is Mormonism? or the question, What is Shintoism? with the same assumption. Such questions as, Is Christianity rational? Is it moral? Is it the ideal religion?, are exceedingly important. Our personal attitude to Christianity is bound up with the answers we give to them. Nevertheless we should endeavor to keep them in the background when we are considering the question, What is Christianity? If we allow them to have a determining influence in deciding what Christianity is, it is highly probable that we will end as Dr. Macintosh ended by seeing in Christianity not the religion founded by Christ and His Apostles but rather a religion that conforms to our personal conception of an ideal religion. Our conception of an ideal religion may conceivably be superior to Christianity but if it is not the same as Christianity we have no right to use the word Christianity to designate it.

In affirming that the question, What is Christianity?, is from first to last an historical question we do not mean to imply that other matters are not involved. The question, What is Christianity?, cannot be dealt with in complete isolation from the question, Is it true? or What is its value? And that because a particular metaphysic, or theory of reality, and a particular epistemology, or theory of knowledge, is implicated in every statement of fact. It is therefore not only unlikely but virtually impossible for the theist and the non-theist to agree as to what Christianity is in distinction from what it claims to be. One may, however, hold to a theistic metaphysic (recognize the existence of two kinds of reality, the created and the uncreated) and a theistic epistemology (recognize two kinds of knowledge, that of the Creator and the creature) without having a correct conception or even any conception of what Christianity is, because Christianity is a product not of speculation but of history. This being the case, the answer to the question, What is Christianity?, can be found in history and in history alone.

Has Christianity Adhered to Type?

It has been much debated whether we are to get our conception of Christianity exclusively from its first century presentation as it finds expression in the teachings of Christ and His Apostles or from its whole historical manifestation. It is clear that Christianity, or at least what has been called Christianity, has had a continuous existence from the first century to the present time. If Christianity did not exist today, few of us would have any interest in the question, What is Christianity? In that case it would, we may be sure, interest most of us as little as the question, What is Mithraism?, though at one time Mithraism was apparently Christianity's chief rival. It is clear, also, that unless Christianity, in some of its historical manifestations, has adhered to its original type, there is no such thing as Christianity in the world today in the early meaning of the word. In that case we would have to distinguish sharply between the Christianity, so-called, of the twentieth century and the Christianity of the first century. If, however, there has been a fundamental type of Christianity that has remained essentially the same in the midst of an ever changing environment and despite many superficial changes of form, if Dr. B. B. Warfield was warranted in saying that "impure as the development of Christianity has been, imperfect as has been its manifestation, corrupt as has often been its expression, it has always presented itself to the world, as a whole, substantially under one unvarying form," [3] there is no good reason why we should not take into consideration not only its primitive form but its whole historical manifestation in determining what Christianity is.

There is relatively little disposition to deny that Christianity as a world phenomenon has adhered more or less closely to type from the time of Paul to the rise and spread of an anti-supernaturalistic Christianity within the last hundred years, that is to say through approximately 1800 of the 1900 years it has been in existence. It is generally admitted that historical or traditional Christianity is essentially one with Paulinism. So outstanding a representative of naturalistic Christianity as Bousset has accused the "orthodox" of "basing the truth of their whole system and the form of their faith on a fantastic, mythical-dogmatic interpretation of the life of Jesus by Paul." [4] What is more, the rank and file of those calling themselves Chris-

[3] *The Person and Work of Christ* (The Presbyterian and Reformed Publishing Co.), p. 307.

[4] *Proceedings and Papers of the Fifth International Congress of Free Christianity and Religious Progress,* p. 209.

tians have never been conscious of any fundamental difference between their own religion and Paulinism. They, like Peter, may find "some things hard to be understood" in Paul's writings but as far as they understand them they find a ready response in their souls. One can hardly read a book like Schaff's *Creeds of Christendom,* which contains the creeds of the Church universal, without realizing that while these creeds may express Paulinism with various degrees of purity yet they are all expressions of Paulinism. Dr. Machen was fully warranted in saying "explain the origin of the religion of Paul and you have solved the problem of the origin of Christianity," [5] provided you have in mind Christianity as it has been professed throughout the Christian ages. If Christianity departed radically from type, it did so before the death of Paul. In that case, they are quite right who maintain that Paul, rather than Jesus, was the founder of Christianity as it has been all but universally confessed and practiced throughout what are known as the Christian centuries.

The real question at issue, therefore, is not whether Christianity as a whole has departed radically from type since the time of Paul but whether, under the influence of Paul and even before and independently of him, Christianity was transformed to such a degree as to change it into a religion of another kind. Those who so maintain—their number has grown rapidly within the last fifty years—tell us that, immediately after the death of Jesus, the religion He taught and exem-

[5] *The Origin of Paul's Religion* (Wm. B. Eerdmans Pub. Co.), pp. 3-4.

plified was modified, re-fashioned, made over, under the influence of the pre-Christian beliefs of His earliest followers and that a still more radical transformation of the "religion of Jesus" occurred when it was altered and even transformed under the influence of the theological constructions of Paul, derived in large part from the Gentiles. As a result, so it is said, it is with what is known as Paulinism that Church history for the most part concerns itself. According to these scholars, two layers of debris must be removed before we can recover the Christianity of Jesus Christ—first that for which Paul is responsible and second that for which the primitive community is responsible. According to these men, Church history has to do, for the most part, with perversions of real Christianity inasmuch as it is only within the last few decades, thanks to modern scholarship, that original Christianity, as taught and exemplified by Jesus Himself, has again come to light.

Did Christianity thus early depart from type? Did the "primitive community," more or less unconsciously, transform the teachings of Jesus into something quite different? Did Paul in turn so alter the teachings of the "primitive community" that he became the real founder of what ever since has been called Christianity by the vast majority of those calling themselves Christians? Paul, were he living today, would certainly repudiate the honor these ascribe to him. Nothing is more certain than that he did not regard himself as the founder of a new religion. He explicitly denied that he preached any other Gospel than that which had been preached before him. What is more, it is safe to say in the light of the most recent scholarship, including Form Criticism, that it has proved impossible to substantiate the alleged difference between Paul and the primitive community on the one hand, and between the primitive community and Jesus Himself on the other. Not only the books of the New Testament as they stand but the alleged sources behind them, whether written or oral, tell us of essentially the same Christ. Not only is the Christ of Paul the same as that of the Gospels, but criticism, whether literary or historical, has failed to find any Christ more primitive than that of Matthew, Mark, Luke and John. The choice at the end of the day is more and more clearly seen to be between the Christ of the whole New Testament and a Christ of whom we have no knowledge whatever. The affirmation of the late James Denney that "Christianity never existed in the world as a religion in which men shared the faith of Jesus, but was from the beginning and amid all undeniable diversities a religion in which Jesus was the object of faith" [6] receives ever stronger confirmation as research, relative to the origin of Christianity, becomes more searching. The only sound conclusion, we believe, is that not only in the mind of Paul and not only in the mind of the "primitive community" but in the mind of Jesus Himself, his-

[6] *Jesus and the Gospel,* p. 12.

torical Christianity is a continuation not a perversion of the religion that He commended.[7]

In view of what has been related it seems clear that the sharp distinction that the naturalists make between historical Christianity and primitive Christianity should not be taken too seriously. To estimate it at its true value we need only keep in mind that it is based not on the actual difference between historical Christianity and Paulinism, or even pre-Pauline Christianity, but between historical Christianity and the Christianity that is found in the early Christian literature after that literature has been so reconstructed or expurgated as to bring it into harmony with naturalistic postulates. While these men professedly contrast historical Christianity and the "religion of Jesus" yet what they call the "religion of Jesus" is about as different from the religion that Jesus actually taught as a religion could possibly be. We would not be understood as alleging that there is no difference between the religion that Jesus founded and which was elaborated by His chosen Apostles, and Christianity as it has manifested itself throughout the last 1900 years—imperfect and degenerate types of Christianity meet us always and everywhere; nowhere do we find absolutely pure Christianity. But we would be understood as maintaining, without fear of successful contradiction, that, despite corruptions and perversions,

[7] See *The Witness of Matthew and Mark to Christ* (1944) by Dr. Ned Bernard Stonehouse.

Christianity has adhered closely enough to type to enable the plain man to see and feel the gulf that divides Christianity and all other forms of religion.

If it be true, as we think is abundantly evidenced, that Christianity, broadly speaking, has adhered to type throughout its historical manifestation, it seems clear that, in seeking to ascertain what Christianity is, we need not confine ourselves to its New Testament manifestation. If we had to choose between getting our conception of Christianity from its New Testament manifestation and its later historical manifestation, we should of course choose the former. As a "founded" religion, Christianity derives its specific content from its founders—Christ and His authorized Apostles. As such, nothing can be regarded as belonging to its essential content which does not appear in the New Testament or can be legitimately deduced therefrom. Not only that, all the later manifestations of Christianity are to be classed as pure or corrupt, adequate or inadequate, according as they conform to this original content. However, while we ought to attach primary significance to the New Testament manifestation in determining what Christianity rightly so called is, inasmuch as all later manifestations are imperfect and some of them rank perversions, yet we ought not to neglect the later manifestations. It is conceivable, no doubt, that at an early date Christianity departed so radically from type that Christianity as a whole is a totally different religion from the religion of the New Testament, but literary and historical criticism fail to support this notion. It may be added that it is impossible to believe that this happened and at the same time believe that the religion of the New Testament is a God-given religion, and its Founder the Son of God. How can it be supposed, on that assumption, that throughout so many centuries His promise of the Spirit, Who would guide His disciples into all truth, was being held in abeyance?

Granted that there has been corruption, is it not reasonable to suppose that there has also been explication? The analogy of what happened in Old Testament times is fitted to suggest that such has been the case. There was much corruption in the Old Testament period. The Israelites violated practically every law given by Moses. They not only persecuted and stoned the prophets but embraced the teachings of the false prophets. And yet side by side with the corruption in teaching and practice so prevalent in that period, not only were additional revelations of the will of God given but there was growth in the understanding of the revelations already given. Whatever the differences between the Old and New Testament periods, we may be sure that, despite corruption, explication and so a better understanding of the nature and significance of Christianity have gone on since its New Testament period. Few if any of us have gotten our conception of Christianity direct from the New Testament uninfluenced by its later historical manifestations. We have no more drawn our conception of Christianity direct from the New Testament than we have drawn our scientific knowledge direct from nature, unaided by text-books, encyclopedias, and such like. Athanasius, Augustine, Anselm, Luther, Calvin, Wesley, not to mention a multitude of others, have not labored in vain. It is because we have entered into their labors that many today have a more adequate conception of Christianity than did the Christians of the second or even of the sixteenth century; and as the years unroll it may be anticipated that our generation will be surpassed in this respect. This is not to deny, rather it is to affirm, that everything presented as an essential of Christianity must be able to present New Testament credentials. At the same time, it is to maintain that actually our conception of Christianity is derived from both its New Testament presentation and its whole historical manifestation. Granted that the New Testament is our original and only authoritative source of knowledge in this matter and that we must be constantly on our guard in considering the later developments lest we look upon perversions or even falsifications of Christianity as being in the line of true development, it is none the less true that we, for the most part at least, have been so largely influenced in our interpretation of the New Testament by the teaching of the existing Churches as expressed in their creeds, and especially as expressed by their accredited teachers, that unless Christianity has adhered more or less closely to type through the changing centuries there is little reason to suppose that there is much real Christianity in the world at the present time.

We have pointed out that in our approach to the question, What is Christianity?, we should ever keep in mind the fact that it is first, last and always an historical question, and that as such the answer to it is to be found in the field of history. This means that it must not be confused with questions having to do with the truth or the value of Christianity and such like. This is widely recognized but often more honored in the breach than in the observance. For instance, to cite a conspicuous example, Harnack in his famous Berlin Lectures entitled *What is Christianity?* began by stating that it was "a purely historical question" with which he was about to concern himself, that "we cannot form any right estimate of the Christian religion unless we take our stand upon a comprehensive induction that shall cover all the facts of history," and that "what is common to all the forms which it has taken, corrected by reference to the Gospel, and, conversely, the chief features of the Gospel, corrected by reference to history, will, we may be allowed to hope, bring us to the kernel of the matter." [8] And yet it cannot be maintained that his discussion of this question is in accord with this profession. Apart from the fact that he does not maintain a purely historical spirit, as evidenced by the naturalistic presuppositions with which he operates, he obviously did not

[8] English Translation, pp. 7, 11 and 15.

utilize the whole phenomenal manifestation of Christianity in arriving at his conception of Christianity but rather made his version of the "religion of Jesus" the touchstone by which to distinguish between what has been rightly called and what has been falsely called Christianity since the days of Jesus. But however poorly Harnack's performance may have conformed to his profession at this point, he has correctly stated the approach we must make to this question, if we are to get the right answer to it. It is the failure of Harnack to adhere to his historical profession which explains the nature of the answer he finally gave to the question we are considering. What is more, we believe that most, if not all, of the wrong or at least inadequate answers being given to this question find their explanation, directly or indirectly, in a similar failure to deal with it as primarily an historical question.

It might be asked, Have we not been guilty of the same error with which we have charged Harnack? This we deny because the supernatural presuppositions with which we have operated are the same as those with which Christ and His apostles, and the adherents of Christianity in general, have operated. On the other hand Harnack has attempted to interpret the history of Christianity in the light of presuppositions to which it has been ever irreconcilably antagonistic.

If men in general would only do what Harnack in his opening lecture indicated that he was going to do, much of the existing confusion, caused by the diversity of things being called Christianity, would rapidly disappear. This would no doubt result in bringing it about that many who now call themselves Christians would no longer do so; but it would put an end to a situation in which many, who reject all that is most distinctive of Christianity rightly so called, look upon themselves as among Christianity's purest confessors and best exemplars and as such its heirs and beneficiaries. There is no good reason why such a situation should exist. It exists, for the most part at least, because due recognition is not given to the fact that the question, What is Christianity?, is from first to last an historical question. What answer does history give to this question? We shall endeavor to indicate what is most central to that answer in the chapter that follows.

"But when the kindness of God, our Saviour, and His love toward man, appeared, not by works in righteousness, which we did ourselves, but according to His mercy He saved us, through the washing of regeneration and renewing of the Holy Ghost, which He poured out upon us richly, through Jesus Christ our Saviour; that being justified by His grace, we might be made heirs to the hope of eternal life. Faithful is the saying, and these things I desire that thou affirm confidently, to the end that they who have believed in God may be careful to maintain good works."—TITUS 3:4-8.

Chapter III

THE ESSENTIAL CONTENT OF CHRISTIANITY

We have pointed out that the question, What is Christianity?, is first, last and always an historical question and that as such the answer to it should be sought in the field of history with as little regard as possible to the question of its truth or falsity or the likes or dislikes of the inquirer. We have further contended that it is the failure to deal with it as such that explains, for the most part at least, the multiplicity and diversity of answers that are being given to this question.

If then, we approach this question as primarily an historical question and look at Christianity in the light of its entire phenomenal manifestation, what do we find? We submit, without fear of successful contradiction, that it will be found (1) that Christianity is a religion that ascribes both its origin and its continuance to the person known as Jesus Christ, (2) that it presents itself as a redemptive religion in the twofold sense that it offers salvation from both the guilt and the corruption of sin, and (3) that it is a religion that sets before its adherents ethical perfection as their goal. The consideration of these points will not serve to bring out the whole of the content of Christianity but it will serve, we believe, to bring out what is most distinctive of it to such an extent as to provide us with a touchstone that will enable us to distinguish with substantial accuracy between Christianity rightly so called and Christianity falsely so called.

The Place of Christ in Christianity

In the first place, Christianity is a religion that ascribes both its beginning and its continuance to the person known as Jesus Christ. Christianity is not the only religion that ascribes its origin to the life, teaching and work of a person—Buddhism and Mohammedanism, to mention no others, do the same—but in no other religion does its founder occupy such a position as Christianity ascribes to Jesus. For Christianity, Jesus is not only its founder, He is also its present head. This difference is basic. For Christianity, Jesus Christ is not merely One who was but One who is, not only One who lived and worked in the past, but One who lives and works today. Christianity has been as dependent upon Him throughout the Christian centuries, is as dependent upon Him today, as in the days of His flesh. Buddha and Mohammed might be forgotten and the religions they founded remain essentially what they are, because the relation they sustain to their followers does not differ in kind from that which Luther sustains to Lutheranism or that which Calvin sustains to Calvinism. In the case of Buddha and Mohammed, the bond that binds their followers together, as in the case of Luther and Calvin, is not so much loyalty to their persons as loyalty to the principles they taught and exemplified. Could they behold what takes place on earth, they would be fully satisfied, assuming that they still think as they thought in the days of their flesh, if they saw the principles they taught ruling the actions of men. It is far otherwise in the case of Christ as He has been and is conceived of in Christian circles. He promised to be with His disciples to the end of the world and desires today, as He desired in the days of His flesh, the love, trust, and obedience of men. He is not satisfied to see men observing the things He commanded, even if they observe them in a spirit of love for others, unless they act out of a consideration for Himself. Paul expressed the mind and hope of Christ for mankind until the end of time, according to Christian belief, when he wrote: "And whatsoever ye do, in word or deed, do all in the name of the Lord Jesus, giving thanks to God the Father through Him" (Col. 3:17). Where Christ is forgotten or ignored, even if His spirit should find exemplification in individuals and even in communities, Christianity does not exist. And that because Christ Himself is Christianity to such a degree that apart from Him as a present object of love and worship, Christianity ceases to be.

According to all but universal Christian belief, at least previous to the spread of what is known as Liberalism or Modernism in recent years, Christ not only points out the way to God; He is the way itself. Herman Bavinck was but giving expression to common Christian belief when he wrote: "The peculiarity of the Christian religion, as has often been shown, and acknowledged even by opponents, lies in the person of Christ. All other religions are independent, to a certain degree, of their founders, because these founders were nothing more than their first confessors But Jesus was not the first Christian; He was and is the Christ. He is not the subject, but the object, of religion. Christianity is not the religion of Jesus, still less Jesus-worship,[1] but Christ-worship. Christianity is now as dependent on Him, from moment to moment, as when He trod the earth. He is not a person who lived and worked only in the past, but He lives and works still, is still Prophet, Priest and King, and Himself upholds the Church, which He established, from age to age, and assures to her the victory. Christianity, according to its own confession, does not exist through the strength and fidelity of its confessors, but through the life and will of its Mediator. The stages of the application of salvation are as much, and in the same sense, His interest as the impetration of salvation. His will and His work is to make men truly religious, to bring them into fellowship with God, and that is also the will and work of God Himself. For the will of God to save the world was not only an annunciation of God's inclination in the past, but is an action, a deed, a work of God, which goes on from day to day. God is love; but that love is no quiescent attribute, but an eternal, omnipresent energy which realizes itself in the hearts of men. God is Father; but that Fatherhood

[1] *i.e.,* Jesusism or the worship of Jesus as a mere man.

is no mere title of honor, but an almighty, energetic power which regenerates men as His children and heirs. Christianity is no mere revelation of God in the past, but it is, in connection with the past, a work in the midst of this and every time. The Father of Jesus works always hitherto, and He Himself works also." [2]

The Place Ascribed to Christ in the New Testament

It hardly requires proof that throughout the New Testament Christianity is represented as a religion that not only had its origin in Jesus Christ but one that would be dependent upon Him for its continuance in the days to come. Wherever we open its pages, we are confronted with a religious life that is grounded in and determined by Jesus Himself. With one voice its writers tell us that Christianity is primarily a personal religion, that at heart it consists not in a system of doctrines or a code of ethics, still less in a system of philosophy or an imposing ritual, but in loving and loyal allegiance to a Person whose rank in the scale of being is one with that of God and as such a proper object of worship and obedience. The latest criticism leaves untouched the contention of James Denney: "Everywhere in the New Testament we are in contact with a religious life which is determined throughout by Christ. Be the difference between the various witnesses what they will, there is no difference at this point. In

2 *The Philosophy of Revelation* (Longmans, Green and Co.), pp. 227-228.

the relations of God and man, everything turns upon Christ and faith in Him. There is no Christianity known to the New Testament except that in which He has a place all His own, a place of absolute significance, to which there is no analogy elsewhere. . . . Christianity never existed in the world as a religion in which men shared the faith of Jesus, but was from the very beginning, and amid all undeniable diversities, a religion in which Jesus was the object of faith. To all believers, Jesus belonged to the divine as truly as to the human sphere. In the practical sense of believing in Him they all confessed His Godhead." [3]

It may not be superfluous, however, to direct attention to a number of New Testament statements that witness to the fact that the first Christians looked upon Jesus as One who continued as an active factor in this world's affairs subsequent to His death. Luke's statement in the opening verses of *The Acts of the Apostles* reflects the viewpoint of New Testament Christians in general. He there states that in his former treatise (*i.e.*, his Gospel) he had dealt with "all that Jesus began both to do and to teach until the day in which He was received up," thus implying that in his present treatise he planned to deal with the things that Jesus had been doing since His ascension. If Luke had himself named the book that he then proceeded to write, there is good reason to think that he would have called it *The Acts of the Risen Christ* rather than *The Acts of the*

[3] *Jesus and the Gospel*, pp. 11-12.

Apostles inasmuch as he ever looks upon the Apostles as but the instruments through whom the living Christ continued to carry on His work in the world. This is in harmony with Christ's final charge to His disciples before His ascension: "All authority hath been given unto me in heaven and on earth. Go ye therefore and make disciples of all the nations, baptizing them into the name of the Father and of the Son and of the Holy Spirit, teaching them to observe all things whatsoever I commanded you: and lo, *I am with you always even unto the end of the world*" (Matthew 28:19-20). That Peter shared Luke's viewpoint is evident from what he says in his First Epistle: "Blessed be the God and Father of our Lord Jesus Christ, who according to His great mercy begat us again unto a living hope by the resurrection of Jesus Christ from the dead . . . whom having not seen ye love; on whom though now ye see Him not, yet believing, ye rejoice with joy unspeakable and full of glory: receiving the end of your faith, even the salvation of your souls" (I Peter 1:3 and 8). It is perfectly obvious that Paul also shared Luke's viewpoint. It was the risen, glorified Christ Who, as he believed, met him on the way to Damascus and in Whose service he was subsequently engaged. For him Christ was ever his living Lord, that One whom God had "highly exalted and given a name which is above every name, that at the name of Jesus every knee should bow, of things in heaven and things on earth and things under the earth, and that every tongue should confess that Jesus Christ is Lord to the glory of God the

Father" (Phil. 2:9-11). We need but add that, for John, Christ was One who could say to His servants, "Fear not; I am the first and the last and the living one; I was dead and behold I am alive for ever more, and I have the keys of death and of Hades" (Rev. 1:17-18) while for the author of the Epistle to the Hebrews, He is One who is "the same yesterday, and today and forever" (Heb. 13:8).

It is this fact that makes the New Testament the most modern, the most up-to-date of all books. It tells not only what Jesus was like in the days of His flesh but what He is like today; not only what His attitude toward men was 1900 years ago but what it is today; not only of the power He wielded then but of the power He wields now; not only of the fact that He received sinners while on earth but of the fact that He receives sinners today. So that He says to men today as truly as He said to those who were His historical contemporaries, "Come unto me, all ye that labor and are heavy laden, and I will give you rest. Take my yoke upon you and learn of me; for I am meek and lowly of heart and ye shall find rest unto your souls" (Matthew 11:28-29). For the Christian, Jesus Christ has ever been not merely One Who lived some 1900 years ago but equally One Who lives today and Who will continue to live until the end of time as the Lord and Life of humanity; and so as One to Whom men can pray, upon Whom they can build their confidence for eternity as well as time and from Whom they can obtain strength and encouragement when as His servants they engage in the battle of life.

It is important in this connection to keep in mind that the New Testament contains no indication of any conflict with regard to the person of Christ. While the Judaizers antagonized Paul at a number of points, there is no evidence that they took any exception to his view of Christ. Had Paul differed at all from the other Apostles at this point, we may be sure that the Judaizers would not have been slow to direct attention to it as evidence that his teaching was other than that of the original Apostles. The lack of any conflict at this point offers conclusive proof that there was no real difference of opinion in the early Church as to whether the religion they proclaimed had its origin and found its continuance in Jesus Christ.[4]

The Place Ascribed to Christ by the Churches

What was true of the New Testament period of Christianity as regards the person of Christ has been largely true of its later historical manifestations, at least in the sphere of confession. It could hardly be otherwise in view of the fact that the Church in all its main organized branches has accepted the New Testament as authoritative. As a result, whether we direct our attention to the creeds of the Churches, their hymns and spiritual songs, or the writings of their representative schol-

[4] See *The Origin of Paul's Religion* by J. G. Machen (Wm. B. Eerdmans Pub. Co.), pp. 355-357.

ars and theologians, we have brought home to us the fact that it has been all but universally recognized that Christianity owes not only its origin but its continuance to the present day to a divine Person Who abides the same through every change and chance of time.

In considering the creeds of the Churches, in this connection, primary significance attaches to the so-called ecumenical creeds such as the Nicene Creed, the Creed of Chalcedon and the Apostles' Creed inasmuch as these have been accepted by all the great branches of the Christian Church—Greek Catholic, Roman Catholic and Protestant alike. The Nicene Creed, the most widely employed of the creeds—the Eastern Church does not use the so-called Apostles' Creed—runs as follows:

> "We believe in one God, the Father Almighty, Maker of heaven and earth, and of all things visible and invisible. And in one Lord Jesus Christ, the only begotten Son of God, begotten of the Father before all worlds, Light of Light, very God of very God, begotten, not made, being of one substance with the Father; by whom all things were made; who for us men and our salvation, came down from heaven, and was incarnate by the Holy Ghost of the Virgin Mary, and was made man; He was crucified for us under Pontius Pilate, and suffered, and was buried, and the third day He rose again, according to the Scriptures, and ascended into heaven; from thence He shall come again, with

glory, to judge the quick and the dead; whose kingdom shall have no end. And in the Holy Ghost, the Lord and Giver of life, who proceedeth from the Father, who with the Father and the Son together is worshipped and glorified, who spake by the prophets. In one holy catholic and apostolic Church; we acknowledge one baptism for the remission of sins; we look for the resurrection of the dead, and the life of the world to come."

It would be easy to collect statements from the later creeds of the Churches—Lutheran, Reformed, Arminian and Wesleyan—in which the same basic view of the person of Christ finds expression. We content ourselves with citing the statement given in the Shorter Catechism of the Westminster Standards (Question 21)—than which there is perhaps no clearer or more succinct statement of the faith of the Church Universal as to the person of Christ. There He is described as "the Lord Jesus Christ, who being the eternal Son of God became man, and so was, and continueth to be, God and man, in two distinct natures, and one person forever." It should be noticed that according to the faith of the Church Universal what Christ was He continues to be. He is not only One who was, but One who is, and who because of His divine nature remains the same yesterday, today and forever.

It would be a work of supererogation to cite the statement of the representative theologians of the Church Universal. Suffice it to say that at this point Aquinas, Luther, Calvin and Arminius are agreed. Theologians who have held lower views of the person of Christ may have had many individual followers but they have never been regarded as representative by any of the great organized branches of the Church. We have to journey to the periphery of Christianity, to sects whose standing in the Christian body is questionable, to say the least, such as the Unitarians, to find an organized body calling itself Christian which does not share the view of Christ that has found such classic expression in the Westminster Standards as cited above.

That Christianity not only had its origin but has its continuance in the living Christ appears with equal clearness if we turn our attention to the hymns and spiritual songs of the Church. From a multitude that might be cited we point to the following:

"My faith looks up to Thee,
Thou Lamb of Calvary, Saviour Divine:
Now hear me while I pray,
Take all my guilt away,
O let me from this day be wholly Thine."

"Jesus calls us o'er the tumult
Of our Life's wild restless sea,
Day by day His sweet voice soundeth,
Saying, 'Christian, follow me.' "

"Jesus, Thou joy of loving hearts,
Thou fount of life, Thou light of men;
From the best bliss that earth imparts
We turn unfilled to Thee again."

Christianity as a Redemptive Religion

We find in the next place that Christianity is a redemptive religion in the sense that it offers salvation from both the guilt and the pollution of sin. There is a sense, no doubt, in which all religions may be called redemptive religions inasmuch as they are, always and everywhere, commended as a means of deliverance from some evil or other, felt as such. But while there is a broad sense in which all religions may be called "religions of redemption," Christianity is basically different from all others in an important respect. It is the only religion that offers redemption in and by the work of another. Other religions, whatever their historical form, assume that men must save themselves. Christianity on the contrary ever maintains that if men are to be saved at all they must be saved by a power outside of themselves, that there is no such thing as a self-saved Christian. Other religions may be rich in moral and spiritual lessons, may abound in wise counsel and good advice, but they appeal to no dynamic, no source of energy other than that which inheres in man as man. But Christianity, rich as it is in moral and spiritual insight and practical wisdom, finds its distinctive note in the fact that it offers salvation in and by the work of Jesus Christ. When we speak of Christianity as a redemptive religion, we do not mean that it is a redemptive religion in the vague sense in which religions in general may be called redemptive but in the particular sense that it offers salvation from sin, conceived as guilt and pollution, through the atoning death of Jesus Christ and through the regenerating and sanctifying influence of the Holy Spirit.

In order to appreciate the sense in which Christianity is a redemptive religion, it is necessary to have in mind the fact that, according to its teaching, sin has brought mankind into a condition resembling that of a man who is both under sentence of death for a major crime and suffering from a virulent cancer. Before such a man could look forward to future earthly happiness and usefulness he would both need to have something done for him and something done in him. To be specific, he would need a pardon from the State and he would need to be cured of his cancer. It would profit him nothing to receive a pardon so long as he was not cured of his cancer just as it would profit him nothing to be cured of his cancer unless he was pardoned for his crime. So is it with the sinner according to Christianity. In the first place the sinner needs something done for him—he needs to be pardoned or forgiven. In the second place he needs something done in him —he needs to be regenerated, sanctified, transformed into a new man. Christianity offers him the first of these benefits through the vicarious life and death of Jesus Christ, the second through the accompanying regenerative and sanctifying operations of the Holy Spirit.

The Significance of the Death of Christ

Christianity is primarily a religion of redemption because it offers salvation from the guilt of sin through the death of Christ as a satisfaction to divine justice. The object of Christian faith has never been Christ *simpliciter* but always Christ *as crucified.* It may even be said that the thought of Christianity as redemptive in this specific sense is more characteristic of Christianity than the thought of it as a religion that ascribes its origin and continuance to Christ, inasmuch as He has always been valued most of all as He who died the Just for the unjust. The deity of Christ is indeed an essential doctrine of Christianity—from the very first it has worshiped Christ as God. This appears not only from the New Testament but from the fact that Pliny in a letter to Trajan, in one of the earliest pagan references to Christianity, stated that the Christians of Pontus and Bithynia worshiped Him as their God. It is, however, not the only essential. It has always been confessed, and not only confessed but placed at the very center of the Christian confession, that apart from His sacrificial death, Christ would not be qualified to be our Redeemer, to grant unto us the forgiveness of our sins and an inheritance among those who are sanctified through faith in Him. While it has always been recognized that all that Christ experienced on earth, all He said and did during that period, contributed toward giving Him the significance that He possesses for men today, at the same time it has always been recognized that what contributed most was His death on the Cross. With Paul, the Church Universal has proclaimed as the most important fact of all that Christ died for our sins. Every great branch of the Christian Church has assigned to His death, regarded as an expiatory sacrifice, the place of primary importance. Greek Catholics, Roman Catholics and Protestants have at least been united in accepting the Cross as the symbol of Christianity and in singing the praises of the "Lamb that was slain."

The capital warrant for attaching such central significance to the death of Christ, needless to say, is to be found in the New Testament. In the Gospels we find that the death of Christ is described with a minuteness that is not paralleled in the account of any other event of His life. Jesus spoke of His death in a way that indicated that He attached supreme importance to it—witness such utterances as: "The Son of man came not to be ministered unto but to minister, and to give His life a ransom for many" (Matt. 20:28); "I am the good shepherd; the good shepherd layeth down his life for the sheep" (John 10:11); "Verily, verily, I say unto you, Except a grain of wheat fall into the ground and die, it abideth alone; but if it die, it beareth much fruit" (John 12:24); "And I, if I be lifted up from the earth, will draw all men unto me" (John 12:32). It is the one event that He commanded His disciples to commemorate (Luke 22:19). If we turn from the Gospels to the Epistles we find, if anything, an even more central significance attached to the death of Christ. Paul declares: "I delivered unto you first of all that which I also received, that Christ died for our sins" (I Cor. 15:3) and "God forbid that I should glory, save in the cross of our Lord Jesus Christ" (Gal. 6:14). Peter writes: "Christ also suffered for sins once, the righteous for the unrighteous, that He might bring us unto God" (I Peter 3:18). John writes: "Hereby know we love because He laid down His life for us" (I John 3:16) and "Herein is love, not that we loved God, but that He loved us, and sent His Son to be the propitiation for our sins" (I John 4:10). The author of the Epistle to the Hebrews writes: "We see Him who hath been made a little lower than the angels, even Jesus, because of the suffering of death crowned with glory and honor" (Hebrews 2:9). So dominant is the place occupied by the death of Christ in the teachings of the Apostles that it is not surprising that some have held that they attach greater significance to the death of Christ than did Christ Himself. Yet in so far as this is the case, it admits of a natural explanation. Christ came "not so much to preach the gospel as that there might be a gospel to preach." In the nature of the case, the full significance of Christ's death could not well have been set forth until after it had taken place.

What was true of Christianity in its New Testament period has also been true, as we have indicated, of its manifestation as a whole. Every important branch of the Christian Church has assigned to the death of Christ a place of central importance. All have freely confessed that apart from His death there would be no forgiveness for sinners. They have not been restrained by the charge that to suppose that Christ received unmerited punishment in order that men might receive unmerited forgiveness is dishonoring to God because it implies that God, the Father, was not disposed to forgive until an atonement had been made. No representation could be more opposed to the truth as they conceived it. So far from seeing in the sacrificial death of Christ that which detracted from its conception of God, the Father, as a God of love, the Church in all its great branches has ever pointed to that death as the supreme proof of the Father's love. It has never reasoned, God is love and therefore there was no need of an atonement. Rather it has always reasoned, God is love and therefore He provided an atonement. "Herein is love, not that we loved God but that God loved us, and sent His Son to be the propitiation for our sins" (I John 4:9-10).

No doubt if the Church of the ages had held the Unitarian point of view, according to which Jesus Christ is but a creature, it would have been as little able as are the Unitarians to see in His death any proof of the Father's love. Nothing is more certain, however, than that it has held the Trinitarian point of view according to which Jesus Christ Himself is the same in substance as the Father. Trinitarians do not suppose that some outside influence had to be brought to bear upon God to lead Him to love sinners. Rather they believe that it was God Himself in the person of His Son who became incarnate for us men and our salvation. Hence they have ever seen in the sacrifice of the Son not only a manifestation of

His love but equally a manifestation of the love of the Father and of the Holy Spirit. They have ever taken at their face value such statements as "God commendeth His love toward us in that while we were yet sinners Christ died for us" (Rom. 5:8) and "God so loved the world that He gave His only-begotten Son that whosoever believeth on Him should not perish but have everlasting life" (John 3:16). It is because Christians have occupied the Trinitarian point of view that they have not permitted themselves to be influenced by the allegation that those who deny there was any need of an atonement to remove obstacles in the way of the exercise of the divine mercy toward sinners have a higher conception of the love of God than those who hold that Jesus by the sacrifice of Himself removed such obstacles. Of course, if God is love and nothing but love, there was no need of an atonement. But if God is a God of holiness and righteousness as well as a God of love, we will be unable to see how He can be just and yet justify the ungodly unless we perceive with Paul that "He justifies them freely by His grace through the redemption that is in Christ Jesus; whom God set forth to be a propitiation through faith in His blood, to show His righteousness . . . that He might be just and the justifier of him that hath faith in Jesus" (Rom. 3:24-26). Surely it ought to be evident to all that just in proportion as we emphasize God's hatred of and detestation of sin, and yet maintain that He Himself provided a propitiation for sin, we give content to our conception of His love. Christians have rejected the Unitarian view not because it embodies too lofty a conception of God as a God of love but because of the inadequacy of its conception of the love wherewith God has loved us.

The thought of the death of Christ as a sacrifice to satisfy divine justice occupies a central place in the creeds of the Churches. The Greek Catholic Church confesses: "He has done and suffered all that is necessary for the remission of sins." The Roman Catholic Church says of the death of Christ: "It was a sacrifice most acceptable to God, offered by His Son on the altar of the cross, which entirely appeased the wrath and indignation of the Father." The Augsburg Confession of the Lutheran Church teaches that Christ "truly suffered, was crucified, dead, and buried, that He might reconcile the Father unto us, and might be a sacrifice, not only for original guilt, but also for all actual sins of men." The Westminster Confession of Faith sums up for the Reformed or Calvinistic Churches when it affirms: "The Lord Jesus, by His sacrifice of Himself hath fully satisfied the justice of the Father, and hath purchased reconciliation for all whom His Father hath given Him." Extracts from the creedal statements of smaller divisions of the Church might be added but these from the main divisions of Christendom should suffice to make clear that, in the later as in the earliest expression of Christianity, supreme importance has been attached to the death of Christ as contributing to that value which He has and will continue to have for the children of men.

The witness of the hymns and spiritual songs of the Church is in full harmony with that of its accredited formularies. Go into any church, unless it be one of the Unitarian or ultra-Modernist ones and it will be found that hymns like the following are in constant use:

"When I survey the wondrous cross
On which the Prince of glory died,
My richest gain I count but loss,
And pour contempt on all my pride."

"There is a fountain filled with blood
Drawn from Emmanuel's veins;
And sinners, plunged beneath that flood,
Lose all their guilty stains."

"Thy life was given for me,
Thy blood, O Lord, was shed,
That I might ransomed be,
And quickened from the dead;
Thy life was given for me;
What have I done for Thee?"

"Come let us join our cheerful songs
With angels round the throne;
Ten thousand thousand are their tongues,
But all their joys are one.
Worthy the Lamb that died, they cry,
To be exalted thus:
Worthy the Lamb, our lips reply,
For He was slain for us."

"Rock of Ages, cleft for me,
Let me hide myself in Thee;

Let the water and the blood,
From Thy riven side which flowed,
Be of sin the double cure,
Cleanse me of its guilt and power."

"Not all the blood of beasts
On Jewish altars slain,
Could give the guilty conscience peace,
Or wash away the stain;
But Christ the heavenly Lamb,
Takes all our sins away,
A sacrifice of nobler name
And richer blood than they."

"Just as I am without one plea
But that Thy blood was shed for me,
And that Thou bidst me come to Thee,
O Lamb of God, I come."

"There is a green hill far away,
Without a city wall,
Where the dear Lord was crucified,
Who died to save us all."

It seems almost superfluous to state that what is true of the New Testament and of the creeds and hymns of the Church is also true of its representative theologians throughout the ages. It would be easy to cull pages of extracts from the outstanding theologians of the past—Augustine, Aquinas, Anselm, Luther, Calvin, Wesley and others—showing the central place that the death of Christ as a sacrifice for sin occupied in their thought and life, but that is hardly necessary. No doubt much of the so-called Christianity of recent years has definitely broken with the idea of the Cross as an expiatory sacrifice for sin. There is no idea seemingly less acceptable to the "modern mind." There are those calling themselves Christians who have not only broken with it but assumed an attitude of open hostility to it. If one were to judge only from the popular literature of the day and from the utterances of many of those religious teachers who have been most successful in gaining the attention of the public, he might even conclude that the idea of the Cross as an expiatory sacrifice for sin is obsolescent if not obsolete. Fortunately, this judgment is not warranted; the doctrine has able defenders in academic circles, is still the common possession of the great majority of those who call themselves Christians. If it were warranted we would be forced to the conclusion that historic Christianity has largely vanished from the earth. For whatever we may think of the truth or value of this doctrine, it is altogether certain that it is a fundamental element in Christianity as it has all but universally been understood by its adherents throughout the Christian centuries. The object of the Christian's faith is and ever has been Jesus *as crucified.* A Christianity that knows nothing of Jesus as crucified for sin has no more right to call itself Christianity than has a Christianity that knows nothing of a Divine Christ. To speak of Christianity without a divine Christ is no more unhistorical than to speak of a Christianity without an atoning Christ.

The testimony not only of the founders of Christianity but of the overwhelming majority of those who throughout the Christian centuries have witnessed the good confession can be cited in support of Warfield who wrote: "Unquestionably, Christianity is a redemptive religion, having as its fundamental presupposition the fact of sin, felt both as guilt and pollution, and offering as its central good, from which all other goods proceed, salvation from sin through the historical expiation wrought by the God-man Jesus Christ. The essence of Christianity has always been to its adherents the sinner's experience of reconciliation with God through the propitiatory sacrifice of Jesus Christ. According to the synoptic tradition Jesus Himself represented Himself as having come to seek and to save that which was lost, and described His salvation as a ransoming of many by the gift of His life, embodying the conception, moreover, in the ritual which He commanded His disciples to perform in remembrance of Him. Certainly His first followers with single-hearted unanimity proclaimed the great fact of redemption in the blood of Christ as the heart of their gospel: to them Jesus is the propitiation for sin, a sacrificial lamb without blemish, and all their message is summed up in the simple formula of Jesus Christ and Him as crucified. Nor has the church He founded ever drifted away from this fundamental point of view, as witness the central place of the mass in the worship of its elder branches, and the formative place of justification by faith in Protestant life. No doubt parties have from time to time arisen who have wished to construe Christianity otherwise. But they have always occupied a place on the periphery of the Christian movement, and have never constituted its main stream.

"We can well understand that one swirling aside in an eddy and yet wishing to think of himself as travelling with the current—even perhaps as breaking for it a new and better channel—should attempt to define Christianity so widely or so vaguely as to embrace him also. The attempt has never been and can never be successful. He is a Christian, in the sense of the founders of the Christian religion, and in the sense of its whole historical manifestation as a world-phenomenon, who, conscious of his sins, and smitten by a sense of the wrath of God impending over him, turns in faith to Jesus Christ as the propitiation for his sins, through whose blood and righteousness he may be made acceptable to God and be received into the number of those admitted to communion with Him. If we demand the right to call ourselves Christians because it is by the teaching of Jesus that we have learned to know God as He really is, or because it is by His example that we have been led into a life of faithful trust in God, or because it is by the inspiration of His 'inner life,' dimly discerned through the obscuring legends that have grown up about Him, that we are quickened to a like religious hope and aspiration—we are entering claims that have never been recognized and can never be recognized as valid by the main current of Christianity. Christianity as a world-movement is the body of those who have been redeemed from their sins by the blood of Jesus Christ, dying for them on the cross. The cross is its symbol; and at its heart sounds the great jubilation of the Apocalypse: 'Unto Him that loveth us and loosed us from our sins by His blood; and He made us to be a kingdom, to be priest unto his God and Father; to Him be the glory and the dominion forever and ever. Amen.' "[5]

Regeneration and Sanctification

We have dwelt at some length on the fact that Christianity is a redemptive religion in the sense that it offers salvation from the guilt of sin through the death of Christ. Sin, however, as we have indicated, involves pollution as well as guilt. It is not enough, therefore, that the sinner be granted pardon. It is equally important that he be freed from his pollution. While it is inconceivable that a righteous God should pardon the sinner apart from an atonement, it is equally inconceivable that a pure and holy God should receive the sinner into His fellowship until, in principle at least, he has become pure and holy. There can be no concord between purity and impurity any more than there can be between light and darkness. If therefore Christianity is to be a redemptive religion in any adequate sense of the word it must deliver the sinner from the pollution of sin as well as from its guilt. It is the glory of Christianity that it does both. The head of a state may pardon a criminal but he has no power to free him of his

[5] *The Person and Work of Christ* (The Pres. and Ref. Pub. Co.), pp. 308-309.

criminal instincts and so cannot guarantee that he will not return to his evil ways. It is otherwise, however, with Jesus Christ. His name was called Jesus because He came to save His people from their sins, *i.e.*, not only from the punishment which their sins as guilt entailed but from sin itself and so also from the pollution and corruption of sin. In order that this may be accomplished the sinner must be regenerated and sanctified, *i.e.*, renewed in the whole man after the image of Christ so that intellectually, emotionally and volitionally he may be spoken of as a new creation.

The work of regeneration and sanctification is in a special sense the task of the Holy Spirit. Christ and the Holy Spirit however never work at cross purposes. They have one aim and ideal. It cannot be said too emphatically that no sinner is pardoned upon whom the Holy Spirit does not operate in a regenerating and sanctifying manner. There is this important distinction, however, to be noted in this connection. While regeneration is an act of God and its effect immediate, sanctification takes place by a process and as such its effects are gradual—a process that in the judgment of many of those calling themselves Christians is never completed on this side of the grave.

Too much stress cannot be placed on this feature of Christianity. It is of equal importance with the fact that it offers salvation from the guilt of sin. While the primary need of the sinner is forgiveness, his ultimate need is purification. Christ being what He is, it is inconceivable that He should be content to obtain forgiveness for sinners while being indifferent to the question whether they be freed from the power and pollution of sin. Great as is the emphasis that Christianity places on the forgiveness of sin as the root of salvation, it places no less emphasis on the cleansing of the heart as its fruit. It never permits the sinner to rest content with pardon as the whole of salvation; it ever strives to make him feel as keenly as possible that salvation comes to its fruition only in a pure heart and a right spirit. No doubt this has not always been adequately stressed. There has been small tendency however in the main stream of Christianity to neglect, still less to deny it—at least theoretically. All types of Christianity that have received expression in the great creeds of the Church insist—some no doubt more adequately than others—that the salvation it promises involves a radical subjective change, wrought by the Holy Spirit, by which tendencies to evil are progressively eradicated and holy dispositions instilled, nourished and perfected.

The difference between Protestants and Greek and Roman Catholics at this point does not concern the absolute need of purification on the part of the sinner but rather the relation between this cleansing of his soul from tendencies to evil and his being received into the divine favor. Both insist on the absolute need of such a subjective change but the former insist, in a way the latter do not, that the sinner does not have to await its realization before being fully restored to divine favor. They maintain that God first receives the sinner into His favor and afterwards makes him worthy of it. According to Protestants in general, God first justifies and then sanctifies the sinner. But they have never supposed that justification is all the sinner needs. They have insisted no less strongly that he needs sanctification, going so far as to maintain that justification cannot be real unless it is followed by sanctification. If they have rejoiced in the possession of the one they have lived in the hope of the other. The fact that they have not taught that salvation is grounded in holiness does not mean that they have not held that its ultimate issue is holiness. However far in the future such a state may seem to be, they have maintained that our completed salvation is nothing less than our perfected sinlessness and holiness.

The most direct opposition to this teaching in the history of the Christian Church took place in the early part of the fifth century under the leadership of Pelagius. Pelagius denied that sin has any subjective effects and so naturally denied that there is need of any subjective operations of God on the souls of men. He held that even after men had sinned they still possessed full ability to do the whole will of God. "I say," declared Pelagius, "that man is able to be without sin, and that he is able to keep the commandments of God." And when he said this he meant that man can do this without the aid of grace in the sense of inward help from God. Pelagius did not deny that men needed "grace" in an outward sense. He saw in the law and the gospel gifts from God which showed men the way of righteousness and which offered incentives to men to walk therein—he even held that Christ by His atoning death had secured forgiveness for past sins—but he denied that sin had wrought any subjective injury on man and affirmed that at any time man by his own initiative and of his own strength could turn from his sin and walk perfectly in the way of righteousness. Under the influence of Augustine, however, the teaching of Pelagius was repudiated and not only repudiated but put once and for all outside the pale of accredited Christian teaching. No doubt there have always been individuals calling themselves Christians who have held in substance with Pelagius but they have been out of harmony with the official teaching of all the great Churches. It is safe to say that there were never so many such, as at present. There are many, including would-be leaders in the historic Churches who out-Pelagian Pelagius. For while Pelagius made a place for expiation as a ground of pardon, these will hear nothing of it. Think of the multitude of those who would have us believe that the Parable of the Prodigal Son contains the very core, even the whole of Christianity, and this despite the fact that it makes no mention of an atonement—not even of Christ or the Holy Spirit. There is no reason to think, however, that this is true of most of those calling themselves Christians. If such were the case it would have to be confessed that Christianity rightly so called has largely disappeared from the face of the earth. Despite its popularity, due to its emotional appeal, all mature Christians know instinctively that W. E. Henley's *Invictus* is Pelagianism or rather paganism unashamed:

> "Out of the night that covers me,
> Black as the pit from pole to pole,
> I thank whatever gods may be
> For my unconquerable soul.
>
> In the fell clutch of circumstance
> I have not winced nor cried aloud,
> Under the bludgeonings of chance
> My head is bloody but unbowed.
>
> Beyond this place of wrath and tears
> Looms but the Horror of the shade
> And yet the menace of the years
> Finds and shall find me unafraid.
>
> It matters not how strait the gate,
> How charged with punishment the scroll,
> I am the master of my fate:
> I am the captain of my soul."

We do not stay to cite the official teaching of the Churches as embodied in their creeds and confessions. However much they may differ in their description of man's state by reason of sin, they all agree, as we have said, that sin involves pollution and corruption as well as guilt and that apart from the regenerating and sanctifying action of the Holy Spirit none of the children of men can become fit for the inheritance of the saints in light. It is not surprising that this is the case—in fact it would be passing strange if it were otherwise—in view of the teaching of Scripture which all recognize as the Word of God and more especially in view of the fact that the Christ in Whom their faith centers affirmed that "except a man be born again he cannot see the kingdom of God" (John 3:3). The Old Testament as well as the New represents sin as involving pollution as well as guilt. Men are represented as shapen in iniquity and conceived in sin and as desiring that God would create a clean heart and renew a right spirit within them (Psalm 51)—a thing that they can achieve by their own efforts as little as the Ethiopian can change his skin or the leopard his spots (Jer. 13:23). It is God who circumcises the hearts of men to love the Lord with all the heart and with all the soul (Deut. 30:6), who puts His law in their inward parts and writes it in their hearts (Jer. 31:33), who takes the stony heart out of their flesh and gives them a heart of flesh that they may walk in His statutes and keep His ordinances and do them (Ezek. 11:19). Isaiah in the presence of the holy God looked upon his uncleanness as sin and felt the need of being purged that he might be worthy of His service (Isaiah 6:5-8). Citations might be multiplied testifying to the fact that throughout the Old Testament dispensation sin was regarded as involving pollution as well as guilt and hence that salvation involved a process of purification as well as expiation.

In the New Testament Christ's unqualified affirmation of the absolute need of a new birth finds abundant confirmation. Paul tells us that we are saved by the washing of regeneration and renewing by the Holy Spirit (Titus 3:5), and speaks of Christians as those who have put on the new man which is renewed in knowledge after the image of Him that created him (Col. 3:10). He beseeches them not to be conformed to this world but to be transformed by the renewing of their minds that they may prove what is that good and acceptable and perfect will of God (Romans 12:2). He urges them to put off the old man which is corrupt according to the deceitful lusts and be renewed in the spirit of their minds and to put on the new man which after God is created in righteousness and true holiness (Eph. 4:22-24). The particular passages cited do not, indeed, exhaust the references in the New Testament that indicate that redemption includes deliverance from the pollution of sin, a transformation after the image of God. This thought underlies and pervades its language. Everywhere the renewal to which those who put their faith in Christ are subjected is represented as a work of the Holy Spirit Who dwells in them as a power not themselves making for righteousness and Who gradually makes them like Christ Himself. Sometimes this is represented as a putting off of the old man and a putting on of the new man (Col. 3:9, Eph. 4:24). Sometimes it is spoken of as a making alive again (John 5:21, Col. 2:13, Eph. 2:4-6) with the result that the Christian emerges as a new creature (Gal. 6:15, II Cor. 5:17). Again it is spoken of as a process of sanctifying or making holy (I Thess. 5:23, Rom. 6:19) and, with a view to emphasizing the function of the Holy Spirit in the process, those subject to it are spoken of as Spirit-led men as distinguished from those who are still carnal, that is their own unregenerated selves (Rom. 8:14, I Cor. 2:14-15, Jude 19). Thus in a variety of ways the Scriptures inculcate the thought that the renewal that is experienced by those rightly called Christians transforms their characters by delivering them from the pollution and so the power of sin and thereby enabling them to walk no longer after the fashion of this world but to prove the will of God, that which is good and acceptable and perfect.

Christianity an Ethical Religion

We have endeavored to make clear that throughout its historical manifestation as a whole Christianity has been presented as (1) a religion that had its origin and finds its continuance in Jesus Christ and (2) that it is a redemptive religion not merely in the general sense in which all religions are such but in the particular sense that it offers salvation from the guilt of sin through His atoning death and from the pollution of sin through the regenerating and sanctifying activity of the Holy Spirit. We have not as yet, however, developed the fact that Christianity is also a religion that sets ethical perfection before its adherents as their goal. We shall touch but lightly on this aspect of Christianity in this connection because we deal with it at some length in the chapter entitled "Christianity and Conduct." Suffice it to say here that it is implicit in what has been said about Christianity as a religion of redemption. It could not be the religion of redemption it is without being through and through an ethical religion.

Good Works

This would seem to be the place to say something about the relation between sanctification and good works. As none are forgiven in whom the process of sanctification is not immediately initiated so none are sanctified in whom sanctification does not issue in good works. As truly as the old unregenerated life manifested itself in works of evil so truly does the new life, originated in regeneration and developed in sanctification, manifest itself in good works. Good works, in a word, are the fruit and the necessary fruit of sanctification. While according to Christian teaching we are not saved by good works—Christ was and is the only Saviour—yet it should not be supposed that men can expect to be saved apart from good works. Indifference to good works evidences the absence of regeneration and sanctification. Such Scriptural passages as the following are typical: "He that abideth in me and I in him the same beareth much fruit" (John 15:5); "For we are His workmanship, created in Christ Jesus for good works, which God afore prepared that we should walk in them" (Eph. 2:10); "The grace of God hath appeared, bringing salvation to all men, instructing us, to the intent that, denying ungodliness and worldly lusts, we should live soberly and righteously and godly in this present world; looking for the blessed hope and the appearing of the glory of the great God and our Saviour Jesus Christ; who gave Himself for us, that He might redeem us from all iniquity, and purify unto Himself a people for His own possession, zealous of good works" (Titus 2:11-14). Such is the emphasis on moral perfection that it is not too much to say that those who do not aspire to it should have nothing to do with Jesus Christ. Why should they seek to employ means that are fitted to bring about ends that they do not desire? If we are to be saved by Jesus Christ we are to be saved not merely from the consequences of sin but from our sin itself. This means that those who are brought into saving contact with Him are destined to become morally perfect, to know a day when all that is sinful has been eliminated from their lives. "Now are we the children of God and it doth not yet appear what we shall be, but we know that when He shall appear we shall be like Him; for we shall see Him as He is. And everyone which hath this hope purifieth himself even as He is pure" (I John 3:2-3). Sanctification, we repeat, expresses itself and cannot but express itself in good works—in conduct after the pattern given us in Christ Jesus. While cleansing from sin begins from within, this inward cleansing will lead to a cleansing of the outside also. There is no escape from the law that every tree produces fruit according to its nature, whether good or bad; hence, if the tree be made good, its fruit will be good while if the tree remain corrupt, its fruit will be corrupt.

It will have appeared that the key-words of Christianity as a world phenomenon are Incarnation, Atonement, Resurrection, Regeneration, Sanctification and Good Works. We proffer the following definition:

Christianity is that ethical religion that had its origin and that has its continuance in Jesus Christ conceived as a God-man; more particularly it is that redemptive religion that offers salvation from the guilt and corruption of sin through the atoning death of Jesus Christ and the regenerating and sanctifying influence of the Holy Spirit.

Men may like or they may dislike such a religion. They may judge it to be rational or irrational, moral or immoral. They may esteem it their chief treasure, that without which they would be poor indeed; or they may look upon it as without value and even as harmful. But be their judgment of it what it may, true or false, moral or immoral, valuable or worthless, we submit that it cannot be intelligently denied—in the presence of those who have the New Testament in one hand and an adequate history of the Christian Church in the other—that as a matter of fact this is what Christianity rightly so called really is.

"In the beginning God created the heaven and the earth."—GEN. 1:1.

"For God so loved the world, that He gave His only begotten Son, that whosoever believeth in Him should not perish, but have everlasting life."—JOHN 3:16.

CHAPTER IV

CHRISTIANITY AND THE SUPERNATURAL

What is the place of the supernatural in Christianity? This did not become a major question until the eighteenth century. Previous to that time there was little disposition to question the reality of the supernatural. "The religious supernaturalistic world-view," as Herman Bavinck rightly affirmed, "has universally prevailed among all peoples and in all ages down to our own day, and only in the last hundred and fifty years has given way to the empirico-scientific."[1] Christianity introduced no change in this respect. Paul differed from the Judaizers at important points in the first century as did Irenaeus from the Gnostics in the second century, but all were supernaturalists. The same was true as regards Augustine and Pelagius in the fifth century. They differed as to whether the supernaturalism of Christianity included "inward grace," but both were supernaturalists. Moreover, the Reformation wrought no change in this respect. Luther and Calvin, as well as the Roman Catholics, were out and out supernaturalists—even the Socinians, the successors of the Pelagians and the precursors of present-day Unitarians, were supernaturalists. In

1 *The Philosophy of Revelation*, p. 1.

those days, and for some time thereafter, one would have looked in vain for one calling himself a Christian who was not a supernaturalist.

The situation has changed greatly since the eighteenth century when there appeared within Christendom a world-view professing to explain the entire world, including man and religion and morality, without the aid of any supernatural factor, purely from resident forces and according to unvarying laws. Nothing indeed is more characteristic of the conception that then made its appearance than its thorough-going naturalism, the resoluteness with which it turns its back on all supernaturalism and the satisfaction with which it claims to find in this world all that thought and life should desire. At first its spread, as was to be expected, was slow but as it found wider and wider acceptance it grew in boldness until it developed, within the last one hundred years, the courage to contest the right of supernaturalism to dominate thought and life any longer. Inasmuch as Christians everywhere continued to stress the supernatural this inevitably led to a repudiation of Christianity. Some of the devotees of this modern world view, believing that Christianity is through and through a supernatural religion, repudiate it altogether. Others of them maintain that while the supernatural has been associated with Christianity historically yet that it does not belong to its essence. These commend a de-supernaturalized or as it is more frequently called a non-miraculous Christianity. It should not be overlooked, however, that the majority of those calling themselves Christians are still out-and-out supernaturalists. They agree with those naturalists who hold that the supernatural belongs to the essence of Christianity but, instead of repudiating Christianity because of this, they repudiate the empirico-scientific world-view inasfar as it can find no place for the supernatural. It is important to keep this in mind if we are to have anything like a right understanding of the existing situation. One could easily get the impression from much current literature that believers in supernatural Christianity constitute but a small minority of those who profess and call themselves Christians. Nothing could be farther from the fact. Whatever may be thought of the supernaturalism of Christianity, it is to shut our eyes to the existing situation to assume that most Christians have given up faith in it.[2]

If we were primarily concerned with the question, Is Christianity true?, it would be incumbent on us to consider the reality of the supernatural. Since we are concerned primarily with the question, What is Christianity?, nothing more is required of us than that we make clear the degree, if any, to which the supernatural enters into the substance of Christianity rightly so called in order that our readers may be in a position to decide between those who maintain that Christianity is through and through a supernatural religion and so one that must be accepted or rejected as such, and those who allege that the supernatural does

2 See pages 12-14.

not belong to the essence of Christianity, and hence something that may be eliminated without causing its destruction.

Can we eliminate the supernatural and still have on our hands anything that can rightly be called Christianity? Obviously this depends on the degree to which the supernatural enters as a constitutive factor into its substance. The degree to which it does this will appear if we enumerate some of the principal ways in which Christianity, as it is set forth in the Bible and as it has found expression in the creeds of the Churches, is committed to the supernatural.

The Christian God

1. In the first place, the God of Christianity is a supernatural God. The Christian never identifies God with nature. Before nature existed, God was, and outside and above and beyond nature, God is. What is more, the richness and fullness of His trinitarian life was enjoyed before nature was brought into existence and would continue to be enjoyed even if nature were annihilated. When the Christian speaks of God he does not, like the pantheist, mean the universe however large it may be conceived to be or however myriad its operations and activities. He means a supernatural God—a God Who is so much greater than the universe that all nature, spiritual as well as material, is in comparison as but the small dust in the balance. It is true that "in Him we live and move and have our being," but it involves a complete rejection of the Christian God to sup-

pose that He lives and moves and has His being in us or in the universe. The God of Christianity is indeed an immanent God but He is above all else a transcendent God—a God so great and of such manifold activities that His immanence in this universe concerns but a small part of His life and activity. It is only as we rise above the thought of the divine immanence and lay hold of the thought that, while God is the God of nature and the God in nature, He is beyond all this the God above nature, that we even begin to know who and what the God of Christianity is. From a Christian point of view, it is to think desperately low of God, is in fact to deny Him, to identify Him with the universe however immensely conceived. It will serve to bring out more fully the sense in which the God of Christianity is a supernatural God if we give some consideration to both the Christian doctrine of creation and the Christian doctrine of providence.

The Christian doctrine of creation involves the notion of a supernatural God. It regards God as the creator of nature, both material and spiritual, and so rejects both the thought that nature is eternal and that it is an emanation from or manifestation of God. It also rejects the theory of evolution as a substitute for the doctrine of creation inasmuch as there must be something to evolve before there can be any evolution, so that the evolutionists must in the end choose between positing the eternity of matter or recognizing a genuine temporal creation. To speak of creative evolution is really a contradiction in terms because what is created is not evolved and what is evolved is not created. The first article of the Apostles' Creed, "I believe in God the Father Almighty, maker of heaven and earth," reflects the opening words of the Bible, "In the beginning God created the heavens and the earth"—words which in various forms find constant expression throughout the Scriptures. In Nehemiah, the priests and Levites address God thus: "Thou, even thou, art Lord alone; thou hast made the heaven, the heaven of heavens, with all their host, the earth, and all things that are therein, the seas and all that is therein" (9:6). The Psalmist addresses God thus: "Lord, thou hast been our dwelling place in all generations. Before the mountains were brought forth, or ever thou hadst formed the earth and the world, even from everlasting to everlasting, thou art God" (90:1-2). In *Acts* we read: "God that made the world and all things therein, seeing that he is Lord of heaven and earth, dwelleth not in temples made with hands" (17:24). In Colossians we read: "For by him were all things created, that are in heaven, and that are in earth, visible and invisible, whether they be thrones, or dominions, or principalities, or powers: all things were created by him and for him" (1:16). The doctrine of creation, the notion that God created all things out of nothing in the sense that He did not use any pre-existing material, is basic to Christian belief and testifies clearly to the fact that the God of Christianity is a supernatural God. Nature according to Christianity is a manufactured article, the product of God's handiwork. He spoke and that which had not been came into existence; and the God who by this act of power brought nature into being is necessarily a supernatural God. No doubt this doctrine of creation is widely denied even by those calling themselves Christians. Such denial, however, does not alter the fact that Christianity maintains that God created the heavens and the earth and that this act of creation was not a mere modification of pre-existing material, still less an evolution or modification of His substance, but that it was an act of creation in the strictest sense of the word.

The Christian doctrine of providence also involves the existence and activity of a supernatural God. According to Christian belief, God not only created the universe, He preserves and governs it by being active in all that takes place in it. Berkhof rightly defines providence as "that continued exercise of the divine energy whereby the Creator preserves all His creatures, is operative in all that comes to pass in the world, and directs all things to their appointed end." [3] The Christian doctrine is opposed to the notion that the universe is governed by chance or by fate. It is also opposed to both Deism and Pantheism. The Deist believes in creation but not that God takes a personal interest in this world's affairs. According to the Deist, the universe is a great machine which God constructed but which operates according to invariable laws. The standard illustration is that of a

[3] *Systematic Theology* (Wm. B. Eerdmans Pub. Co.), p. 106.

clock and, since according to the Deist, the universe is a good clock, it can be depended on to accomplish the ends it was designed to accomplish. The Deist is opposed to chance and caprice but he makes everything and every person cogs in a great machine. According to the Christian conception, however, God's relation to the world is rather that of a pilot to a ship. The Christian conceives of the universe as being under the control of a Person—a Person all of Whose actions are governed by intelligent purpose. It is even more opposed to Pantheism. Since Pantheism identifies God and the world, it leaves no room for creation and, since it denies the personality of God, it cannot believe in providence in anything like a Christian sense. While Christians have differed widely in their conception of the control that God exercises over the universe He has created they are at one not only in rejecting the notion that the universe is ruled by fate or chance but in repudiating Deism and Pantheism in any of their consistent forms. Doubtless there have been individual Christians who have skated close to Deism or Pantheism in their efforts to explain divine providence but it has been generally recognized that the Christian conception of providence cannot be made to fit into a Deistic or Pantheistic scheme of things. The divine preservation of all things is clearly taught in Scripture (Matt. 10:29, Acts 17:28, Col. 1:17, Heb. 1:3). God's activity in all things is also clearly taught and more often implied (Acts 17:28, Eph. 1:11) and God's control and guidance of all things repeatedly stressed

(Acts 17:24, Rev. 19:6, Dan. 4:34-35, Matt. 10:29-31). Many other references could be cited but these will suffice to make clear that only a supernatural God could exercise such providential control as Christianity posits.

Christianity and Miracles

2. In the second place, the God of Christianity is a God who has intervened supernaturally in the affairs of this world. The Deist believes in a supernatural God Who created this world but not in a God Who has intervened in the sense of acting directly in its affairs since He first created it. This means that the Christian, unlike the Deist, believes in the supernatural in the form of the miraculous.

The possibility of the supernatural in the form of the miraculous is given in the Christian doctrine of God as a supernatural God. In the nature of the case if God created and sustains and governs this universe, the possibility of His intervening in its operations cannot be denied. No doubt there is a presumption against His doing so. Some think that the presumption against His interfering with the operation of the laws which He has established is so great that no evidence can be strong enough to prove that He has done so. Christians deny this. They hold rather that the presumption is in favor of such action on God's part in view of the moral and spiritual condition in which sin has brought mankind. If the human race were in a normal condition, morally and spiritually, there would be a strong presumption against the supposition that God has intervened in a miraculous way. But if the human race is in an abnormal condition, morally and spiritually, if it has gone wrong, so seriously wrong that it is a lost and condemned world, then for those who believe not only in a supernatural God but in a God who is interested in the welfare of His creatures, the presumption may well be in favor of the notion that He will intervene, that He will stretch forth His hand to save and redeem. Be that as it may, Christians rightly so called believe not only in the possibility but the actuality of supernatural acts subsequent to the creation of this universe and the establishment of the laws according to which it ordinarily operates.

Those who believe in the existence of a supernatural God Who not only created but Who sustains and governs this universe, in the manner already indicated, are Theists. But a Theist is not necessarily a Christian. All Christians are Theists but not all Theists are Christians. We are Christians only if we believe that God has intervened supernaturally through the person and work of Christ to save sinners from the guilt and corruption of sin and to make them meet to dwell in the presence of a God Who is of purer eyes than to behold evil and can not look upon iniquity. It is within the sphere of the miraculous that we come face to face with that which is most distinctive of Christianity. No doubt there have been many attempts to provide us with a non-miraculous Christianity. It may be safely said, however, that they have all ended in failure. This has not been due to any lack of ability on the part of those making the attempt. They have included in their number thinkers and scholars of the first rank. It is due to the fact that in attempting to give us a non-miraculous Christianity they have been attempting the impossible. And that because the choice is not between a miraculous and a non-miraculous Christianity but between a miraculous Christianity and no Christianity at all. Deny the supernatural in the form of the miraculous and the statement of John 3:16 is without any basis of fact. Then there is no warrant for affirming that "God so loved the world that He gave His only begotten Son that whosoever believeth in Him should not perish but have everlasting life."

Without pretending to indicate all the ways in which the supernatural in the form of the miraculous enters into the substance of Christianity, let us consider some of the more outstanding ways in which it does this. When we do this we find that miracles are basic to Christianity both when they are defined in a narrow and when they are defined in a broad sense. When defined in a narrow sense, miracles are events in the external world wrought by the immediate power of God. When defined in the broader sense, they include acts and works of God wrought in the spiritual world. In the narrow sense, miracles are confined to such events as the virgin birth and bodily resurrection of Jesus Christ or such of His deeds as the raising of Lazarus, walking on the water and feeding the five thousand. But when taken in the broad sense, miracles also include such things as regeneration and sanctification. Most of the debate over miracles has had to do with miracles defined in the narrow sense, as these most obviously contravene the naturalistic world view, but it should never be forgotten that regeneration, justification and sanctification are as much supernatural acts and works of God as any that have taken place since the dawn of creation. To perceive the constitutive place of miracles in Christianity we need remember no more than that they include (1) those great acts of redemption that God has wrought for the salvation of men—acts which culminate in the life, death and resurrection of Jesus Christ, (2) the supernatural interpretation of those events recorded in the Scriptures, (3) the supernatural appropriation by sinners of the benefits of those events through the regenerating and sanctifying activity of the Holy Spirit and (4) those events which are to take place in the future in connection with Christ's return and the consummation.

There are many miracles in the narrow sense of the word, indicated above, recorded in the Scriptures. These miracles are confined, for the most part, to four widely separated periods, (1) the deliverance of the Chosen People from Egypt and their establishment in Palestine under Moses and Joshua, (2) the life-and-death struggle between the religion of Jehovah and Baal worship in the time of Elijah and Elisha, (3) the manifestations of the power and supremacy of Jehovah over the gods of the heathen at the time of the Babylonian Captivity and (4) the time of the establishment of Christianity in this world by Christ and His Apostles. The great majority of them are recorded in connection with the fourth period. Including the miracles of healing, between thirty-five and forty are recorded in the Gospels alone and a smaller number in the *Acts of the Apostles*. There is, also, frequent mention of general manifestations of miraculous power so that the total impression given is that the miracles recorded are but specimens of the whole number performed. The fact that these miracles are confined almost exclusively to these critical periods in the history of the religion of the Bible shows that they were not performed arbitrarily. It harmonizes with the notion generally held by Christians that they were performed in the interest of the economy of redemption, *i.e.*, it has been generally held that it was the entrance of sin into this world that made the supernatural intervention of God in the course of world events necessary if sin was to be destroyed and the creation renewed to its pristine glory. In harmony with this we note that these miracles find their culmination in the life, death and resurrection of Jesus Christ conceived of as a divine being Who came to seek and to save that which was lost.

In considering these miracles, it is important to observe that they are not mere appendages to

Christianity—something like a porch to a house that can be removed without destroying or even seriously injuring the main building. If miracles merely prefigured or symbolized Christianity or if their value were purely evidential or their purpose merely to authenticate the Prophets and Apostles and even Jesus Himself as messengers from God—all of which they are—it could not be claimed that they enter into the very substance of Christianity to such a degree that apart from them there could be no such thing as Christianity rightly so called. Then the advocates of a non-miraculous Christianity would be able to justify their contention. But such is not the case. It is of course true that all the miracles recorded in Scripture are not essential to the same degree. Conceivably many of them might never have happened or not have been recorded and yet Christianity be essentially what the Church of all ages has regarded it as being. No one supposes, for instance, that Christianity stands or falls with the question whether an ax floated in the days of Elisha or whether Jonah was swallowed by a whale or whether Lazarus was raised from the dead or whether Jesus fed five thousand with five loaves and two fishes. These as well as many other miracles recorded in the Scriptures might not have been reported by the Biblical writers and Christianity be essentially what it is. But while that is true, there are other miracles recorded in the Scriptures which are essential to the very existence of Christianity—miracles the elimination of which would leave Christianity but a mass of ruins, or rather miracles apart from which there would never have been such a thing as Christianity. We refer to such miracles as the incarnation and the resurrection of Christ from the dead. Such miracles cannot possibly be classed as non-essential. They enter in a constructive way into the substance of the Christian religion; they are indispensable to its very existence. With such miracles in mind it is perfectly proper to say that Christianity denuded of its miracles is something other than Christianity and as such should be called by another name.

That, as regards Christianity, the choice is between a miraculous Christianity and no Christianity at all, appears most clearly when it is perceived that we cannot eliminate the miraculous without eliminating Jesus Himself. Jesus Himself is the greatest of all miracles. It is He who stands at the center of Christianity and makes it what it is. One might as well suppose that the Pope could be eliminated without destroying Roman Catholicism as an organization, nay more, that the sun could be removed from the heavens without destroying our solar system, as suppose that we can get rid of the person of Jesus Christ and still have left anything that can rightly be called Christianity.

It is miracles of this sort that supply the factual basis of Christianity. A mighty series of facts that find their center in the incarnation, atonement, resurrection and heavenly priesthood of Jesus Christ are basic to Christianity as it has found expression in the New Testament and throughout the history of the Christian Church. It cannot be stated too strongly or too frequently that Christianity is grounded in facts, in events that happened in space and time. Whoever rejects these facts or minimizes their importance, whether he realizes it or not, is an enemy of the Christian religion. The declaration of Lessing, so often quoted by those who commend a non-miraculous Christianity, "accidental truths of history can never be the proof of necessary truths of reason," consistently applied, tears up Christianity by the roots inasmuch as Christianity derives its distinctive content not from "necessary truths of reason" but from what Lessing calls "accidental truths of history." No doubt this exposes Christianity to the perils of historical investigation. A religion that confines itself to eternal truths is independent of historic facts and so may be unconcerned about the historicity or unhistoricity of any alleged event. It is quite otherwise, however, with Christianity. It stands or falls with the question whether certain events actually happened. Apart from these events, it would have no gospel. For "gospel" means "good news," information about something that has happened. Basic to Christianity are those great acts of redemption that God has wrought for the salvation of His people—acts that either center about or find their culmination in the birth, life, death and resurrection of Jesus Christ. Yet these facts are miraculous in nature. Hence if the miraculous is ruled out they are ruled out with it.

The great majority of those calling themselves Christians—all, we are disposed to say, who have an intellectual right to call themselves such—have believed or do believe in miracles in the narrow sense of the word. There has not been and is not, however, the same unanimity of opinion concerning the question whether miracles, in this sense of the word, still occur. There are many, including the Roman Catholics, who hold that such miracles are wrought in our own day and generation. The great majority of Protestants, however, hold and have held that the function of miracles in this narrow sense, except in as far as they enter into the substance of Christianity in a constitutive way, was to authenticate the organs of revelation, particularly the Prophets and Apostles, as authoritative messengers from God. And hence that not only the need but the working of such miracles ceased with the passing of the Apostles and the establishment of Christianity in the world.

But while Christians have differed concerning the reality of miracles in the narrow sense of the word, subsequent to the passing of the Apostles and those upon whom they bestowed this gift, there has been a marked unanimity among them as to the continued occurrence of miracles in the broad sense of the word. No doubt there are important differences here as to the mode of operation of the Holy Spirit in regenerating and sanctifying those whom Christ saves—according to Roman Catholics, for instance, the Holy Spirit employs the Church and the sacraments in a different manner from that which He does according to Protestants—but they one and all hold that men stand in need of regeneration and sanctification to such a degree that apart from them they cannot become the recipients of eternal blessedness and that neither is possible apart from the supernatural work of the Holy Spirit. There are also important differences as to the absoluteness of the sinner's dependence upon the supernatural work of God in order to obtain salvation. Pelagius, early in the history of the Church, denied that men need the inward help of God to achieve their salvation, affirming that men have the ability to meet all their obligations and so are able to be without sin and able to meet all the demands of God. Under the influence of Augustine, however, the Church rejected, once and for all, this denial of "grace" in the sense of inward help from God and affirmed that "we are aided by the grace of God, through Christ, not only to know but also to do what is right, in each single act, so that without grace we are unable to have, think, speak, or do anything pertaining to piety." [4]

It is true that since that time there have been many calling themselves Christians who have followed Pelagius rather than Augustine—never so many as at the present time. However they have not only always been but are still out of harmony with the official teaching of the organized churches, unless we recognize churches of the Unitarian type as genuinely Christian Churches—something which even so inclusive an organization as the

[4] *Council of Carthage,* 417-418 A.D.

Federal Council of the Churches of Christ in America has as yet shown itself unwilling to do. It is true also that the Augustinian doctrine of the grace of God has not been maintained in its purity in most sections of the Church with the result that for the most part the majority of those calling themselves Christians have occupied a position somewhere between Augustinianism and Pelagianism—a position known as Semi-pelagianism. Nevertheless, there has never been a recognized branch of the Christian Church in which the absolute need of "grace," in the sense of inward divine help, has not been acknowledged. It is safe to say that Warfield spoke not only for himself but for the Church Universal when he wrote: "It is not enough to believe that God has intervened in this natural world of ours and wrought a supernatural redemption: and that He has Himself made known to men His mighty acts and unveiled to them the significance of His working. It is upon a field of the dead that the Sun of righteousness has risen, and the shouts that announce His advent fall on deaf ears: yea, even though the morning stars should again sing for joy and the air be palpitant with the echo of the great proclamation, their voice could not penetrate the ears of the dead. As we sweep our eyes over the world lying in its wickedness, it is the valley of the prophet's vision which we see before us: a valley that is filled with bones, and lo! they are very dry. What benefit is there in proclaiming to dry bones even the greatest of redemptions? How shall we stand and cry, 'O ye dry bones, hear ye the word of the Lord!' In vain the redemption, in vain its proclamation, unless there come a breath from heaven to breathe upon these slain that they may live. The redemption of Christ is therefore no more central to the Christian hope than the creative operation of the Holy Spirit upon the heart: and the supernatural redemption itself would remain a mere name outside of us and beyond our reach, were it not realized in the subjective life by an equally supernatural application." [5] The work of the Holy Spirit in sanctification must be distinguished from His work in regeneration. The latter involves a new birth, the implanting in the sinner of a new principle of life, whereas the former has to do rather with the growth and development of that new life and so with the process by which the holy disposition created in regeneration is strengthened and its proper manifestations increased. In the nature of the case there can be no cooperation between the Holy Spirit and the sinner in regeneration, but in sanctification there is constant cooperation. In each case, however, according to common Christian belief, the supernatural work of the Holy Spirit is absolutely indispensable.

Eschatological Miracles

What we have said is more than enough, we believe, to make clear that the supernatural in the form of the miraculous occupies a large and determinative place in Christianity. But an important matter is still to be mentioned. Anything like an adequate perception of the place of the

[5] *Biblical and Theological Studies* (The Presbyterian and Reformed Publishing Co.), p. 19.

supernatural in Christianity can be had only by those who take into consideration those manifestations of the miraculous that are scheduled to take place in the future. Eschatology, the doctrine of the last things, is such an essential part of Christianity that Dr. Geerhardus Vos has rightly said that "a so-called Christianity that is cold or hostile towards the interests of the life to come has ceased to be Christianity in the historic sense of the word." [6] This means that the supernaturalism of Christianity cannot be conceived at its height unless we take into consideration its teaching as to the future, particularly its teaching as to the consummation.

It is clearly taught in the Scriptures and the creeds of the Churches that Christ is to come again in visible form, that the unnumbered millions that have peopled the earth are to be resurrected, and that at the end of history stands the judgment seat of Christ where men shall be assigned their eternal destinies according as they have done good or evil. Christians differ and have differed as to the events that will precede and follow the personal return of Christ—there are a-millennialists, pre-millennialists and post-millennialists—but they have been and are united in accepting at their face value the words spoken by the angels to the men of Galilee immediately after Jesus ascended: "Ye men of Galilee, why stand ye looking into heaven? this Jesus who was received up from you into heaven, shall so come in like manner as ye beheld Him going into heaven." (Acts 1:10.) No doubt

[6] *Pauline Eschatology*, p. 63.

there are those calling themselves Christians who have no faith in such a return of the Lord but at the best they are poorly instructed and at the worst they are Christians falsely so called.

We are interested in calling attention to the return of Christ, the resurrection of the dead, and the consummation in this connection only to direct attention to the supernaturalism which they necessarily involve. It is not too much to say with Dr. Vos that "eschatology is supernaturalism in the *n*th degree." [7] If its doctrine of the last things were but an appendage to Christianity, something that could be lopped off without affecting it in any substantial way, Dr. Vos' statement would be a gross exaggeration. Such, however, is not the case. Eschatology has been rightly called the "crown and capstone" of theology without which all its questions would have at the most but a partial answer. For instance, as Berkhof points out, were we to ignore eschatology, we could not say how the disrupting influence of sin will be completely overcome, how the work of Christ will be crowned with complete victory, how the work of the Holy Spirit will issue in the complete redemption and glorification of the people of God or how God will finally be completely glorified and His counsel fully realized.[8] What we are more particularly concerned to point out, however, is that manifestations of the supernatural, surpassing any that have been made, are to take place in connection with

[7] *Pauline Eschatology,* p. 62.
[8] *Systematic Theology* (Wm. B. Eerdmans Pub. Co.), p. 665.

the consummation according to Christianity in the historic sense of the word.

We have not enumerated all the ways in which the supernatural is implicated in Christianity but surely we have said enough—more will be said in later chapters—to make clear that it enters into its very essence. It may be that having shown in the preceding chapter that Christianity is a redemptive religion that had its origin and that ascribes its continuance to Jesus Christ conceived as God incarnate, there was little or no need of evincing that Christianity is a supernatural religion. Because, in the nature of the case, such a religion is through and through a supernatural religion. However, in view of the anti-supernaturalistic atmosphere in which men live today and the influences beating upon them fitted to lead even Christian men and women, if not to deny the supernatural, at least to confess as little of it as possible, it would seem that there is some need of reminding the men and women of our generation of the kind and measure of the supernatural recognized not only by Christ and His Apostles but by the Church Universal since their departure. We have made clear, if we mistake not, that the supernatural enters into the substance of Christianity to such a degree that Christianity de-supernaturalized is Christianity divested of all that makes it a source of hope and comfort to the children of men.

"For I delivered unto you first of all that which I also received, that Christ died for our sins according to the Scriptures, and that He was buried, and that He rose again the third day according to the Scriptures."—I Cor. 15:3-4.

Chapter V

CHRISTIANITY, FACTS AND DOCTRINES

Christianity, as we have defined it, is based upon and constituted by certain factual and doctrinal elements. There are those who object to our conception of Christianity on one or both of these grounds.

There are those who deny that Christianity stands or falls with the actuality or historicity of any facts. Christianity, they claim, is independent of facts—facts being at the most but symbols or illustrations of the truths that are constitutive of Christianity. These hold that Christianity consists of doctrines not facts. There are others who maintain nearly the opposite of this. Their watchword is: Christianity consists of facts not doctrines. Doctrines, according to these, are little if anything more than epiphenomena that accompany the facts and as such are at the most of secondary importance. But whatever the significance these attach to doctrines they deny that any specific doctrines enter in a constitutive and so essential way into the formation of Christianity. There are still others who deny that either facts or doctrines are constitutively essential to Christianity. Their watchword is: Christianity is life, not facts or doctrines. Since all three of the viewpoints indicated are widely held and far reaching in their implications, no one of them may be ignored by those who are concerned to make clear to the men and women of our generation what Christianity rightly so called is. Let us consider them in the order named.

Doctrines Not Facts

1. In the first place, there are those who object to our definition of Christianity because of the importance it attaches to historical facts. These deny that such facts belong to the essentials of Christianity; they maintain rather that Christianity and historical facts have little or nothing to do with each other. The classical period of this point of view is that of the Enlightenment of the eighteenth century and its classical expounder, Gotthold Ephraim Lessing (1729-1781), whose famous declaration, "accidental truths of history can never be the proof of necessary truths of reason," supplied what may be regarded as its watchword.

What commends this view to many today is its claim to give us a Christianity that is independent of historical criticism. As such it is a fruit of historical scepticism. If Christianity is independent of historical facts, it is obvious that it is a matter of no great moment at what conclusions literary and historical criticism may arrive as to the historical truthfulness of the Bible. Those who deny that Christianity rests upon and is constituted by historical facts differ as to the degree to which it is the fruit of divine revelation; but all are agreed that what matters is "truth of idea" rather than "truth of fact." They are interested in facts only in as far as they are the outward expression of some idea or principle. They all share Immanuel Kant's notion that facts of history are but symbolic representations of eternal truth.

This view is much more widely held than most people suspect. It is implied if not openly confessed whenever and wherever men identify Christianity with love or morality or altruism or brotherhood or such like. It is the view of all mystics, at least those who spell mysticism with a capital M. The out-and-out Mystic no more than the out-and-out Rationalist can attach any essential significance to historical facts. In the nature of the case those who live solely by what they find within themselves—whether they stress the emotional or the rational element—can attach no decisive significance to external facts of history. And so we find Mystics calling themselves Christians who sublimate the entire body of facts recorded in the Bible into a series of symbols that dramatize the psychological experiences of the soul. Both Rationalists and Mystics are sworn enemies of the historical and in as far as they call themselves Christians cannot but advocate a Christianity that at heart consists exclusively of eternal truths and not at all of historical facts, real or alleged.

In view of the wide prevalence of the notion that Christianity is independent of facts, whatever be the explanation, it is not surprising that some hold that Christ Himself occupies no essential place in the religion that He founded. For Christ belongs to history and to maintain that facts are not essential to Christianity is to maintain that Christ Himself is not essential. If, then, we deny that facts are constitutive of Christianity, we cannot call ourselves Christians without being advocates of a Christless Christianity or at least of a Christianity in which Christ's position is no more essential than Plato is to Platonism. Those who accept this view should at least do so realizing that it commits them to a religion that can, if necessary, get along without Christ. The difference between those who maintain and those who deny that facts are essential to Christianity has been well expressed by Dr. Geerhardus Vos: "The difference between those who can do without the facts and us who feel we must have the facts, does not lie on the periphery of the Christian faith: it touches what to us is the center. It relates to nothing less than the claim of our holy religion to be a supernatural religion, and a religion which objectively saves from sin. . . . Let us suppose for a moment that our religion aimed at nothing more than a disclosure of a system of truth for the spiritual enlightenment of mankind—that there were no sins to atone and no hearts to regenerate and no world to transform. In that case its connection with historical facts would have to be regarded as a purely incidental matter, established for the sake of a more vivid and effective presentation of the truth, and therefore separable from the essence of the truth itself. Obviously, further, it would on this supposition be of no consequence whether the historical mould into which the truth was cast consisted of a record of actual events or of mythical and legendary lore having only a partial basis of facts, or a conscious literary fiction having no basis of facts at all. The same will apply to every view of religion which makes the action of the truth consist exclusively in the moral suasion exercised by it on the human mind. . . .

"To the Christian Church in the most catholic sense of the word, supernatural religion has always stood for something more than a system of spiritual instruction or an instrument of moral suasion. The deep sense of sin, which is central to her faith, demands such a divine interposition in the course of the natural development as shall work actual changes from guilt to righteousness, from sin to holiness, from death to life, in the sphere not only of consciousness but of being. Here revelation is on principle inseparable from a background of historic facts with which to bring man's life into vital contact, is indeed the main reason for its existence. He who has once clearly perceived this will not even for a moment consider the possibility that his faith and such criticism as destroys the supernatural facts can peacefully dwell together in the same mind. To him the facts are the very bread of life. Though you tell him a thousand times that the value of the Biblical narratives for moral and religious instruction remains precisely the same whether the facts occurred or not, it will not satisfy him, because he knows full well that all moral instruction and religious impressions combined cannot save his soul. In his thirst for redemption from sin he will not rest in anything short of an authentic record of how God wrought wonders in history for the salvation of His people.

"History we need, and that not only in the form of a tale of a certain perfect ethical and religious experience, which has somewhere come to the surface on the endless stream of phenomena, but such history as shall involve the opening of the heavens, the coming down of God, the introduction of miraculous regenerative forces into humanity, the enactment of a veritable drama of redemption between the supernatural and the natural world. Whether we like it or not, criticism can touch the essence of our religion, because religion has become incarnate, and for our sakes had to become incarnate and make itself vulnerable in historic form. As the Son of God while on earth had to expose Himself to the unbelief and scorn of men, so the word of the Gospel could not be what it is for us unless it were subject to the same humiliation." [1]

Facts Not Doctrines

2. In the second place there are those who object to our definition of Christianity not because of the emphasis it places on facts but because of the emphasis it places on doctrines. Their position is almost, if not altogether, the exact opposite of the one we have considered. Their contention is that Christianity consists of facts not doctrines. We would be the last to deny that Christianity is both

[1] *Christian Faith and the Truthfulness of Bible History,* Princeton Theological Review, July 1906, pp. 298-300.

based upon and constituted by certain great facts —such as the incarnation, the atonement and the heavenly high-priesthood of Christ—and if it were necessary to distinguish as sharply as the advocates of this view would have us do between facts and doctrines, we would find the essence of Christianity in its facts rather than its doctrines. We contend, however, without fear of successful contradiction, that it is impossible to do this. Instead of saying that Christianity consists of facts not doctrines we should rather say that it consists of facts and *therefore* also of doctrines. The doctrines are the interpretations of the facts. Apart from their interpretation the facts are meaningless and wholly lacking in significance. A fact without a doctrine is simply a fact not understood. As James Denny once put it: "A fact of which there is absolutely no theory is a fact which stands out of relation to everything in the universe, a fact which has no connection with any part of our experience; it is a blank unintelligibility, a rock in the sky, a mere irrelevance in the mind of man. There is no such thing conceivable as a fact of which there is no theory, or even a fact of which *we* have no theory; such a thing could not enter *our* world at all; if there could be such a thing, it would be so far from having the virtue in it to redeem us from sin that it would have no interest for us and no effect upon us at all." [2]

Dr. James Orr, writing in similar strain, said: "Christianity, it will be said, is a fact-revelation— it has its center in a living Christ and not in a

[2] *Studies of Theology,* p. 106.

dogmatic creed. And this in a sense is true. . . . The gospel is no mere proclamation of 'eternal truths,' but the discovery of a saving purpose of God for mankind, executed in time. But the doctrines are the interpretation of the facts. The facts do not stand blank and dumb before us, but have a voice given to them and a meaning put into them. They are accompanied by a living voice which makes their meaning clear. When John declares that Jesus Christ is come in the flesh and is the Son of God, he is stating a fact, but he is none the less enunciating a doctrine. When Paul affirms 'Christ died for our sins according to the Scriptures,' he is proclaiming a fact, but he is at the same time giving an interpretation of it." [3]

It is safe to say, therefore, that a Christianity that rests upon and is constituted by facts will necessarily be a doctrinal Christianity seeing that facts to become objects of religious contemplation must pass through the doctrinal alembic. The watchword, "Christianity consists of facts not doctrines" should therefore be replaced by the watchword, "Christianity consists of facts and therefore of doctrines." Give the facts no interpretation and they are meaningless and as lacking in significance as though they were completely unknown. The reason why this is not always recognized lies, no doubt, in the fact that those whose watchword is, "Christianity consists of facts not doctrines," do not really mean "bare facts" but rather facts accompanied by a measure of interpretation, *i.e.,* it

[3] *The Christian View of God and the World,* p. 25.

is the fact as interpreted and not the bare fact itself that they call a fact. They speak, for instance, of the fact of the atonement but such a statement involves doctrine inasmuch as it involves an interpretation of Christ's death as atoning for sin. Or they speak of the fact of the incarnation but the word "incarnation" carries with it an interpretation of the person of Christ as a manifestation of the divine in the sphere of the human. Provided the word "Christ" is not taken as referring to a super-human person it is, perhaps, to state a "bare fact" to say that He died on the Cross but we cannot say as much as that He died for our sins without passing beyond "bare fact" and entering the realm of interpretation or doctrine. If those who maintain that Christianity consists of facts not doctrines would only strip the facts so bare that they would be facts and nothing but facts, it would soon become clear to them, it seems to us, that such facts contain nothing that make them constitutive of Christianity or even of anything for that matter.

No doubt it is frequently alleged that the Bible contains merely a record of the facts that constitute Christianity. It is quite obvious, however, that such is not the case. Whatever one may think of the authority of the Bible, it cannot plausibly be denied that it also contains interpretation. Take for instance Christ's death. It cannot be reasonably denied that when Christ Himself spoke of giving His life "a ransom in the place of many" and of His blood as covenant blood "shed for many unto the remission of sins" that He was interpreting for His disciples the meaning of His death. It is equally unreasonable to deny that the Pauline letters are largely concerned with the interpretation of the incarnation, death and resurrection of Jesus Christ. It is quite unintelligible to say that such statements as the following made by Paul and others, "Christ died for our sins according to the Scriptures"; "Christ was once offered to bear the sins of many"; "He loosed us from our sins by His blood"; "He is the propitiation for our sins"; and "Behold the Lamb of God that taketh away the sins of the world" express a fact but not a doctrine, still less a fact as opposed to a doctrine.

Neither Facts Nor Doctrines

3. We have directed attention both to those who maintain that Christianity consists of doctrines not facts and those who maintain that it consists of facts not doctrines. We come now, in the third place, to call attention to those who deny that it is constituted by either facts or doctrines. The watchword of this group—a very large one—is that Christianity consists of life not doctrine. While the watchword says nothing about facts, yet those who employ it do not hesitate to affirm that Christianity consists of neither facts nor doctrines. Even if they did not do this, it would be implied inasmuch as a factual Christianity is, as we have shown, necessarily a doctrinal Christianity.

It is true, it is needless to say, that Christianity is a life—a life that is lived in communion with the Son of God. The whole series of Christian facts as well as the whole body of Christian doctrines exist in order to make possible this life. Christ did not become incarnate, live as He lived during the days of His flesh, and die on the Cross and rise again merely that He might insert so many extraordinary facts into the ordinary course of history. The creation of the facts was not an end in itself. The purpose of His action was that men might have life and that they might have it more abundantly. And the interpretation of the significance of these facts was given us not merely to add to our fund of knowledge, but for the specific purpose of making us wise unto salvation. What is more, though the series of facts and doctrines which constitute the sum of Christian knowledge is in order that men might have life and have it abundantly, it is not within the power of knowledge by itself to create life. The Christian life is not created by the facts or the doctrines of Christianity but by the workings of the Holy Spirit in the hearts of men. However, from the fact that Christianity is a life, and that a knowledge of the facts and doctrines of Christianity has no power of itself to create this life, it does not follow that a zeal for Christian doctrines is a zeal for a sterile intellectualism. Granted that such zeal may exist where the life is wanting, it does not follow that the Christian life can exist, still less thrive, where knowledge of the Christian doctrines is wholly absent. Unless it does follow, one can be indifferent to the doctrines only as he is indifferent to the distinctively Christian life.

No doubt there is a sense in which it is true that life precedes doctrine, *i.e.*, an understanding of the facts constitutive of Christianity. Otherwise Paul would not have written that "the natural man receiveth not the things of the Spirit of God, for they are foolishness to him; and he cannot know them because they are spiritually judged" (I Cor. 2:14). It is true that apart from the aid of the Holy Spirit dwelling within them, men cannot apprehend the things of God. If this is all that is meant when it is alleged that Christianity is life not doctrine, it would have the fullest approval of all intelligent Christians. There is, as we have said, no creative power in doctrines, however true; and as such the knowledge of them may leave souls as dead as though they were unknown. It is the creative activity of the Holy Spirit which alone is capable of quickening dead souls into newness of life, so that apart from Him all the doctrines in existence will not produce one spark of life. This, however, is not what is meant by those who employ this watchword. What they mean is that life precedes doctrine not only in importance but in time, more particularly they mean that doctrine is only a product of life. In the nature of the case this assigns to doctrines a place of secondary importance. It does not deny the right of Christian doctrines to exist. Rather it affirms that wherever there is Christian life there will be Christian doctrines as the interpretation of the life. But the doctrines will not be looked upon as the condition of the life and as the determiner of its form but as the fruit or product of the life and as such only a manifestation of the previously existing life. The steps are as follows: first there is the life; the life issues in action; one form of the action being intellectual, doctrine will be a result. According to these, the life does not manifest itself differently according to doctrine but doctrine alters as the life of which it is the expression alters. This, we submit, does not explain why the life of the Mohammedan or the Buddhist or the Fetish-worshipper differs from that of the Christian.

The historic explanation is that the differences in living between Christians and non-Christians are to be accounted for by the different doctrines or religious conceptions that prevail in these different circles. If the historic explanation be the true explanation, it is not true that life precedes doctrine in the sense intended. Rather doctrine precedes life and is the cause of the particular form in which the religious life manifests itself in these different circles. If this be the case, then it follows in turn that to be indifferent to the distinctive doctrines of Christianity is to be indifferent to the distinctive form in which the life manifests itself in Christian circles. Here the words of the French scholar, M. Henri Bois, are much to the point: "Doctrine is of little importance, what is of importance is life, we are told. But, it being admitted that life is the essential thing—a matter which is as incontestable as it is uncontested, and which when it is admitted, saves us from Intellectualism in the only censurable sense of the word—the question is precisely whether certain doctrines are not necessary for the production and maintenance of a certain life. Doctrines are not life! Assuredly not. No one ever said they were. But does it follow that they are not indispensable to life? Doctrines are not the cause of life! On that we are agreed. Does it follow from that that they are not one of the conditions of life?"

It must be admitted that the watchword, "Christianity is life not doctrine," is not in harmony with the view held by the founders of the Christian religion. This appears most clearly, perhaps, in the writings of Paul. With him it is ever first the doctrine and then the life. The Epistle to the Romans is typical. Eleven chapters of doctrine precede five chapters of precepts. Between them stands one of his significant "therefores." "I beseech you *therefore* brethren"—"therefore" because of and in view of the doctrines expounded in the first eleven chapters they should live as exhorted in the last five. Nothing could indicate more clearly his conception of the relation between doctrine and life. What was true of Paul was true of the other Apostles and, what is more significant, true of their Master before them. Never did He or His Apostles teach or imply that the good seed is unnecessary for a desirable harvest or that the unsowed soil, however good, is capable of producing such a harvest. Knowledge of God's will was ever represented as the condition of doing God's will, sound doctrine as being at the root of all good conduct and all true religion.

Both Facts and Doctrines

4. All possible views are held concerning the extent to which facts and/or doctrines enter into the essence of Christianity. Some, as we have just seen, hold that neither enter in a constitutive way; some, that doctrines but not facts, while others, that facts but not doctrines, enter into Christianity in this way. There are others, however, who hold that both facts and doctrines enter into the make-up of Christianity to such a degree that where either is lacking there is no such thing as Christianity rightly so called. According to this fourth group—they include the great majority of those who have called themselves Christians to date—it is quite impossible to distinguish as sharply between facts and doctrines as two of the groups mentioned would have us believe. And that because, as we have already contended, unless facts are interpreted, *i.e.*, converted into doctrines, they are meaningless and might, for all practical purposes, not exist. These hold, therefore, that a Christianity which rests upon facts must necessarily be a doctrinal Christianity. They do not deny that there may be doctrines that have no basis in fact but such are to be classed at best with myths and legends and at worst with lies—and there are no Christians, they take it, who are concerned to maintain that doctrines of that sort are

essential to Christianity. They put the matter thus. Give the facts no interpretation and they are meaningless. Give them an interpretation other than that which the New Testament gives them and they yield us something other than Christianity. It is only when we accept the interpretation that the Biblical writers give them that they yield us what can rightly be called Christianity.

It will be seen, in view of what has just been said, that the conception of the relation between facts and doctrines, commonly held in Christian circles, involves the notion of an authoritative Bible. The writers of Scripture never imply, either directly or indirectly, that the interpretation of the facts they record is merely the result of their human reflection upon them. They claim that the interpretation of them which they present was given them immediately by God and hence that the meaning they have ascribed to them is their meaning for God—hence their true meaning. If we regard them as untrustworthy in their interpretation of the facts which lie at the basis of the Christian religion, is it possible for us to regard them as trustworthy in their report of the facts themselves? The two are so inextricably bound together that to question one is, perforce, to question the other. If we reject the interpretation which the Biblical writers place upon the recorded supernatural events recorded by them we shall be hard put to it to justify the belief that the events themselves were other than natural events. It cannot be said too emphatically that Christianity, as it has most widely been understood, is based upon and constituted not only by the facts recorded in the Scriptures but equally by the interpretation placed upon those facts by the Biblical writers. Any and all attempts to distinguish between the facts of Christ's life as the permanent divine element in Christianity—to confine our attention for the moment to that which is most central—and the interpretation of those facts as the human and so relative and changing element, necessarily assumes that the interpretation given us in the New Testament is nothing more than human reflection on those facts. In that case the interpretation merely gives us their meaning for men—a meaning which may be far removed from that which God places on them. This means that a revelation by deeds unaccompanied by words of explanation would fall short of our needs. More broadly expressed, this means that we cannot do away with the idea of external authority in religion and still possess a well-grounded assurance that we have an adequate Christianity—any Christianity at all for that matter. Deny that the Scriptures constitute an external authority and we shall be in doubt not only as to the right meaning of the facts recorded in them but of the occurrence of the facts themselves.

Protestants and Catholics differ as to the seat of authority. The former locate it exclusively in the Bible or rather the Holy Spirit speaking in the Bible; the latter locate it in the Bible plus tradition as interpreted by an allegedly infallible Church. The same general presuppositions, however, underlie both views, *viz.*, that general revelation has been supplemented by a special revelation in Christ through Prophets and Apostles, and that adequate provision has been made for preserving and propagating saving truth. It is a mistake of the first order to identify the Protestant doctrine of private judgment with free thought, the rejection of all authority in matters of religion. It is in the Italian freethinkers and in the Socinians, not in Luther, Calvin and Zwingli, that the Rationalists of the age of the Reformation are to be found. Protestantism, apart from the so-called New Protestantism current in Liberal and Modernist circles, is committed to external authority in its doctrine of the Scriptures as truly as are the Roman Catholics in their doctrine of the Church. Reject the idea of external authority and both would suffer irreparable injury.

It is a matter of first importance for the understanding of Christianity to realize that it is based upon and constituted by deeds of God as authoritatively interpreted by the Biblical writers. "There is nothing more important in the age in which we live," it has been rightly said, "than to bear constantly in mind that all the Christianity of Christianity rests precisely on 'external authority.' Religion, of course, we can have without 'external authority,' for man is a religious animal and will function religiously always and everywhere. But Christianity, no. Christianity rests on 'external authority,' and that for the very good reason that it is not a product of man's religious sentiment but is a gift from God. To ask us to set aside 'external authority' and throw ourselves back on what we find within us alone—call it by whatever name you choose, 'religious experience,' 'the Christian consciousness,' 'the inner light,' 'the immanent Divine'—is to ask us to discard Christianity and revert to natural religion. Natural religion is of course good—in its own proper place and for its own proper purposes. Nobody doubts, or nobody ought to doubt, that men are by nature religious and will have a religion in any event. The *sensus divinitatis* implanted in us, to employ Calvin's phrases, functions inevitably as a *semen religionis*.

"Of course Christianity does not abolish or supersede this natural religion; it vitalizes it, and confirms it, and fills it with richer content. But it does so much more than this that, great as this is, it is pardonable that it should now and then be overlooked. It supplements it, and, in supplementing it, it transforms it, and makes it, with its supplements, a religion for and adequate to the needs of sinful man. There is nothing 'soteriological' in natural religion. It grows out of the recognized relations of creature and Maker; it is the creature's response to the perception of its Lord, in feelings of dependence and responsibility. It knows nothing of salvation. When the creature has become a sinner, and the relations proper to it as creature to its Lord have been superseded by the relations proper to the criminal to its judge, natural religion is dumb. It fails just because it is natural religion and is unequal to unnatural conditions. Of course we do not say that it is suspended, we only say that it has become inadequate. It requires to be supplemented by elements which are proper to the relations of the offending creature to the offended Lord. This is what Christianity brings and it is because this is what Christianity brings that it so supplements and transforms natural religion as to make it a religion for sinners. It does not supersede natural religion; it takes it up in its entirety unto itself, expanding it and developing it on new sides to meet new needs and supplementing it where it is insufficient for these new needs. . . . Valuable as is the inner light—adequate as it might be for men who were not sinners—there is no fate which could be more terrible for the sinner than to be left alone with it. And we must not blink the fact that it is just that, in the full terribleness of its meaning, which Mysticism (and Rationalism) means. Above all other elements of Christianity, Christ and what Christ stands for, with the Cross at the center, come to us solely by 'external authority.' No 'external authority,' no Christ and no Cross of Christ." [4]

Current Doctrinal Indifferentism

Only as we understand the relation between the facts and doctrines of Christianity and the degree to which both are constitutive of Christianity can we estimate rightly the doctrinal indifferentism that is so characteristic of the age in which we live. Much of this doctrinal indiffer-

[4] Warfield, *Biblical and Theological Studies* (The Pres. and Ref. Pub. Co.), pp. 455-458.

entism is exceedingly superficial resting on no firmer basis than an innate dislike for clear thinking or the fact that this and that good man rejects this or that doctrine which other Christians regard as an essential Christian doctrine. The superficiality of this latter contention is indicated by the fact that "good" men can be found who severally reject practically every doctrine of Christianity, and hence it logically implies that no doctrines are essential. It is no answer to this to say that essential not unessential doctrines are in mind because, if any doctrines are essential, doctrinal indifferentism cannot be justified. Admit the existence of any essential doctrines and doctrinal indifferentism stands condemned. There may be a legitimate difference of opinion as to whether this or that doctrine is essential but there can be no legitimate indifference to doctrines as such. However, by no means all of the doctrinal indifferentism of the day is of this superficial character. As we have seen some of it is based on the notion that Christianity consists of facts not doctrines and some of it is based on the notion that Christianity consists of life not facts or doctrines. If doctrinal indifferentism is to justify itself at all, there is little doubt but that it must employ the latter method. And that because, as we have indicated, it is impossible to have facts without doctrines. Only if it can be maintained that Christianity consists of neither facts nor doctrines can doctrinal indifferentism be successfully defended. If, however, both facts and doctrines belong to the very essence of Christianity, it is obvious that doctrinal indifferentism on the part of Christians cannot possibly be justified. Christians may differ among themselves as to what doctrines are necessary but none with any adequate conception of what Christianity is can be doctrinal indifferentists.

"I have been crucified with Christ; and it is no longer I that live, but Christ liveth in me: and the life which I now live in the flesh I live in faith, the faith which is in the Son of God who loved me and gave Himself for me."—GAL. 2:20.

CHAPTER VI

OBJECTIVE AND SUBJECTIVE CHRISTIANITY

Christianity, as we have defined it, has both an objective and a subjective aspect. It is an objective reality in as far as it derives its content from what is external to man, more particularly in as far as it is dependent upon the Person and work of Jesus Christ. It is a subjective reality in as far as it enters into the hearts and lives of men as manifested in what is known as conversion and sanctification issuing in holy living. There can be no adequate conception of Christianity where both of these aspects of Christianity are not given due recognition. Despite this fact, there are those calling themselves Christians who place the whole, or at least almost the whole, of the emphasis upon one or other of these phases of Christianity.

There are those, in the first place, who put an exclusive or at least too exclusive emphasis on objective Christianity. The most flagrant representatives of this group are those known as Antinomians. On the basis of a misinterpretation of the text, "Ye are not under law, but under grace" (Rom. 6:14), they allege that the believer is free from any obligation to obey the law. Some have gone to the extreme of maintaining that "good works are hurtful to salvation." While but few have gone to that extreme there have been a considerable number who have maintained that the work of redemption was finished by Christ in such a sense that nothing remains for the Christian to do. No doubt the total number of professed Antinomians in the history of the Christian Church has been relatively small. It can hardly be denied, however, that the number of those who have more or less fully exemplified their principles in practice has been regretfully large. The words of the once well-known revival hymn beginning with the stanza, "Nothing great or small, Nothing, sinner, no; Jesus did, did it all, Long, long ago" and containing the words, "Lay your deadly doing down, Down at Jesus' feet: Doing is a deadly thing; Doing ends in death" can be understood not as a warning against the supposition that men can save themselves by their own efforts but as an encouragement to cherish the false idea that they can be saved no matter what kind of lives they live. It may be accounted fortunate, therefore, that its use has been largely discontinued.

Elsewhere we point out the inadequacy of any conception of Christianity that is unconcerned about its subjective side.[1] We content ourselves in this connection with calling renewed attention to the fact that it gives no proper recognition to the teaching of Scripture that Christ came to save His people *from* their sins, *i.e.,* not merely from the consequences of their sins but from sin itself. To suppose that objective Christianity is the

[1] See pages 76 ff.; also the chapter on "Christianity and Conduct."

whole of Christianity is to imagine that sin involves guilt only, that it has wrought no subjective injury in the form of corruption which renders the sinner incapable of himself to be and do what he must be and do if he is to be fit for the Kingdom of God. It is true that in view of our guilt our primary need is forgiveness. None the less, forgiveness alone would not suffice. A radical transformation of character, such as is possible only as we are freed from the corruption of sin, is a precondition of our entrance into the Kingdom of God (John 3:5). Hence the Christian doctrine of salvation is radically misunderstood unless it is perceived that it includes a radical subjective change wrought by the Holy Spirit in the sinner by means of which evil tendencies are gradually eradicated and holy dispositions introduced, nourished and perfected. It cannot be said too frequently or too emphatically that the salvation which Christianity offers is a salvation which includes salvation from the corruption of sin through the regenerating and sanctifying activity of the Holy Spirit. This being the case, what we have designated objective Christianity cannot possibly be anything like the whole of Christianity.

There are others who place the emphasis on subjective Christianity to such a degree as to deny —some expressly, others by inference—that there is such a thing as objective Christianity. The number of those who do this today is very large. It may, in fact, be said to be the dominant view in Liberal and Modernist circles. The late Professor George Cross of Rochester Theological Seminary expressed it thus: "Christianity exists nowhere but in Christians. They *are* Christianity." [2] More recently two of the outstanding representatives of this circle have given expression to essentially the same view. Dr. Charles Clayton Morrison, late editor of *The Christian Century*, affirms that "the Christian Church is Christianity" and that "this living community is Christianity, and nothing else is." [3] Dr. Harris Franklin Rall, Professor of Systematic Theology at Garrett Biblical Institute, defined Christianity "as the ongoing life of that fellowship which had its origin with Jesus and seeks its continuous inspiration and guidance in him, finding through him the God of its faith, the goal of its hope, and the way of life." [4] Many others might be cited to the same effect. This view is inherent in the position of all those who identify Christianity with some moral or spiritual quality of character like morality or altruism or loyalty or Christlikeness. It is also inherent in the position of those who define Christianity as "the religion of Jesus," meaning the religion that Jesus Himself practiced. If we identify Christianity with any quality of character or define it in such a way as to make Jesus Himself little if anything more than the first Christian, it is obvious that we can think of Christianity as existing only as these particular qualities of character manifest themselves in human lives or only as men believe and

[2] *What Is Christianity?* (The University of Chicago Press), p. 194.
[3] *What Is Christianity?* (Willett, Clark and Co.), pp. 68 and 317.
[4] *Christianity: An Inquiry into Its Nature and Truth* (Charles Scribner's Sons), p. 57.

act as Jesus believed and acted. It is true that wherever Christianity is a living religion such qualities of character are, in some degree, in evidence. It is true also that where Christianity is in evidence men believe and act in some degree as Jesus believed and acted except in as far as Christians make Jesus the object of their faith (in the nature of the case Jesus did not stand in a religious relation toward Himself) and except in as far as certain of His actions were possible only to a divine being. It is not true, however, that such beliefs, practices and qualities of character constitute the whole of Christianity. To so assert is to ignore the difference between the apples that appear in the market and the trees upon which they grew. It is not indifference to, or an underestimation of, the value of these things that leads us to maintain that Christianity is not to be identified with them, but rather the conviction that they are not found in genuinely Christian form save as they are the product of objective Christianity.

The question whether subjective Christianity is the whole of Christianity is bound up with the question whether external facts, events in history, enter into the substance of Christianity. Those who deny that Christianity is based upon and constituted by such facts may be free to maintain that subjective Christianity is the whole of Christianity, but not those who affirm that they do. For the latter, Christianity necessarily has an objective as well as a subjective side. The reality of objective Christianity is involved in the historic conception of Christ. If we looked upon Christ as merely a great or even the greatest of earth's moral and spiritual teachers and exemplars, we could think of Christianity as existing only as He finds imitators, only as His teaching and example find expression in the lives of men. But inasmuch as we look upon Him as more than a teacher and example, as One Who is also a Saviour Who in order to qualify for that role had not only to live a perfect human life but to suffer death upon the Cross, it is quite impossible for us to look upon subjective Christianity as the whole of Christianity. Wherever Christ is the object of faith there is necessarily such a thing as objective Christianity.

We have pointed out that those who deny or minimize the importance of subjective Christianity are more or less blind to the corruption of sin. We need not admit that those who place virtually the whole emphasis on subjective Christianity have an adequate conception of the corruption of sin in order to maintain that they are blind to its guilt. Guilt calls for atonement and atonement, in the very nature of the case, involves more than pardon. It involves an actually wrought expiation as a fact or event that occurs in time and place. Since Jesus Christ by His atoning death has made it possible for God to be just and yet justify the ungodly—as Christian teachers of all ages, Paul in the forefront, have taught—it is certain that there is an objective element in Christianity rightly so called.

In the light of what has been said, we repeat that Christianity has both an objective and a subjective aspect. We should not permit ourselves to be diverted, or rather led astray, either by those who place too exclusive an emphasis on objective Christianity or by those who place too exclusive an emphasis on subjective Christianity. If we had to choose, it would perhaps be better to go with those who know nothing but subjective Christianity— as there is no heresy worse than the heresy of Antinomianism—but both commend defective versions of Christianity which should be avoided as plagues of the worst sort. Both are fatally one-sided. It should be kept constantly in mind that Christianity has both of these sides and that any adequate conception of what it is, and what it involves, is impossible unless due recognition is given to both. Granted that objective Christianity fails of its purpose if it does not issue in subjective Christianity, it is at the same time true that apart from objective Christianity there is not and cannot be anything that can properly be called subjective Christianity. Here as much as anywhere the exhortation "what God has joined together, let not man put asunder" is relevant. One apart from the other is either valueless or impossible. These two are parts of one whole, organically united like a tree and its fruit.

How closely related to or rather how dependent subjective Christianity is upon objective Christianity appears with special clearness when it is noted that, looked at from the divine side, it is the result of the application to the individual of the salvation wrought out by Jesus Christ while, looked at from the human side, it is the result of the appropriation of the finished work of Christ by the individual. Obviously, before objective Christianity can be applied or appropriated there must be such a Christianity to apply or appropriate. How then could there be such a thing as subjective Christianity if there were no such thing as objective Christianity? Conceivably, objective Christianity might be a reality with a complete absence of subjective Christianity, *i.e.*, it is conceivable, however unlikely it might be, that the Son of God should have taken upon Himself the flesh of our humanity, have lived, taught, suffered and died as a sacrifice for the world's sin, risen from the dead and returned to the glory which He had had with the Father before the world was, and thereby qualified Himself to save men from both the guilt and power of sin, without this resulting in the actual salvation of any of the children of men. It is not even conceivable, however, that there should be such a reality as subjective Christianity, rightly so called, if there were no such thing as objective Christianity. That would be to suppose that we can have an effect without a cause, that, for instance, we could have oranges and apples if there were no orange and apple trees. Christianity in as far as it is objective, more explicity in as far as it consists of the Person and work of Jesus Christ, became a reality in the fullness of time in order that there might be such a thing as subjective Christianity, *i.e.*, that men and women might be saved—not only saved from the guilt and corruption of sin but re-made after the likeness of Jesus Christ in knowledge, righteousness and holiness.

Individual and Collective Manifestations of Christianity

Subjective Christianity manifests itself both individually and collectively. In the individual, it manifests itself in repentance, faith, conversion and sanctification issuing in holy living. Of these, faith—not faith as a state of mind or faith in general but specifically faith in Jesus Christ—is the more pivotal as it is the proximate source or instrumental cause of the others. Apart from such faith there is no repentance, conversion or sanctification in the Christian sense of these words. At the same time subjective Christianity manifests itself collectively. There is no such thing as a completely isolated individual Christian. Whether we will or not, "none of us liveth to himself and no man dieth to himself." The human race is an organism. It does not consist of a vast number of individuals related to one another as the grains of sand that lie upon the seashore. Rather it consists of a multitude that no man can number who are bound together as the cells of the human body. Try as he may, the individual cannot escape from this fact—even the anchorites did not wholly succeed. It is the family rather than the individual that is the unit of society in the divine economy. Moreover, as the individual is a member of a family so the family is a member of a larger group like the community, and this in turn of a still larger group like the state or the nation, and so on until the whole race is embraced. Restricted more immediately to the matter at hand, this means that under normal conditions the individual Christian is a member of the Church and of society. There is, it is true, a considerable difference of opinion among Christians as to the dependence of the individual Christian upon the Church as an organization in this connection. Roman Catholics are not alone in holding that the Church as an organization is the means or instrument of originating and nurturing subjective Christianity in such a sense that outside the Church as an organization it does not exist. Protestants in general, however, while holding that the Church as an organization is a means of grace do not maintain that membership in it is absolutely necessary to the existence of subjective Christianity, desirable and even mandatory as such membership is. But however much Christians may differ in their estimate of the function of the Church as an organization, it is safe to say that they are agreed that all Christians belong to the Church as the body of Christ and that outside the Church in this sense there is no salvation. However much the majority of them may disagree with Calvin in many respects, they are not disposed to take exception to his declaration that "the Church is the mother of all those who have God as their Father." [5]

[5] *Institutes of the Christian Religion.* Book IV, Chap. 1.

Since Christianity manifests itself, not only individually in faith, repentance, conversion and sanctification issuing in holy living, but collectively in the Church and in society at large, Christians are or should be evangelists not only in the narrow sense of endeavoring to lead others to become Christians but in the broad sense of creating a society permeated and dominated by Christian principles and ideals. There are those who interpret this obligation to evangelize too narrowly, those who act more or less fully on the assumption that to be converted and to convert others is the whole of Christian duty. It may be granted that this stands high among Christian duties. Evangelism in the narrow sense of the word is the deepest and most lasting service, even from a purely earthly viewpoint, that one man can render another. Other forms of benevolence may feed the hungry and clothe the naked. Evangelism makes men capable of feeding and clothing themselves by touching the springs of manhood and self-respect and transforming them from within. And while it does this on a small scale in the case of individuals it, at the same time, does it on a large scale in society at large in as far as it does it in individuals. In the light of history it can be said that wherever the light of the Gospel shines, the blessings of civilization abound also. Christ's final charge to His followers ere He returned to that glory which He had had with the Father before the world existed was: "Go ye therefore and teach all nations, baptizing them in the name of the Father, and of the Son, and of the Holy Ghost: teaching them to observe all things whatsoever I have commanded you" (Matt. 28:19-20). In the nature of the case men cannot have regard to *all the things* Christ commanded without being centers of influence that make for social well-being. Though it is true that Jesus put the emphasis on the conversion and sanctification of the individual, His ultimate objective was the conversion and sanctification, so to speak, of society itself. His aim and purpose for this world will not have been realized until out of the sinful members of our race there have been produced not only Christlike men and women but a society in which justice shall prevail, in which love shall be the law and happiness the portion of all. It is quite unwarranted to suppose that because Jesus placed the primary emphasis on the redemption of the individual He is indifferent to social conditions. Rather we should see in this emphasis, evidence that He is wisely concerned inasmuch as the redemption of the individual is the condition of the redemption of society. There is, it is true, much difference of opinion among Christians as to details. Premillennialists, Amillennialists and Postmillennialists conceive of the matter somewhat differently but, despite their differences, they are agreed that ultimately there is to be a redeemed society.

We have directed attention to the close relation between subjective and objective Christianity. We now direct attention to an important difference between them. While the former is in constant flux, the latter remains the same through every change of chance and time. Objective Christianity has to do with what God has done for us men and our salvation, the provision He has made for our redemption. It is a finished thing. Its specific content was given it once and for all by Christ and His Apostles. It has remained the same through all the Christian centuries and will remain the same at least until Christ comes again. Concretely expressed, objective Christianity has to do with Jesus Christ as He sits at God's right hand, fully equipped to save unto the uttermost all those who come unto God through Him. He has not changed with the passing years. He remains "the same yesterday, and today, and forever." It is objective Christianity that Jude had in mind when he spoke of "the faith which was once for all delivered to the saints." It is otherwise, however, with subjective Christianity. Whether viewed individually or collectively it varies from time to time. There are "babes in Christ" and there are those who approximate to full grown men. There are communities once markedly pervaded by the spirit of Christ in which that spirit is now all but absent. There are other communities from which this spirit was once wholly absent which are now largely pervaded by it. In the case both of individuals and of communities there is not only "first the blade, then the ear, then the full corn in the ear," there are also flood tide and ebb tide, periods of progress and periods of decline.

Objective Christianity, as must have appeared, has to do primarily with the question, What is Christianity? Subjective Christianity, however, as must have also appeared, has to do rather with the question, What is a Christian? Closely related as are these two questions, they are by no means identical as those who make subjective Christianity the whole of Christianity would have us believe. These to the contrary notwithstanding, it is one thing to say what Christianity is and another thing to say what a Christian is. While there could be no such thing as a Christian if there were no Christianity, it is at least conceivable that there could be such a thing as Christianity without there being any Christians. And even if it be held that, in view of the promises of God, it is impossible to believe that Christianity should exist without there being any Christians, the existence of Christianity carries with it no assurance that this or that individual is a Christian. Just as there is a difference between the questions, What is Buddhism? and What is a Buddhist? so there is a difference between the questions, What is Christianity? and What is a Christian?

But while these two questions are by no means identical, they are so intimately related that the answer we give to the question, What is Christianity? necessarily determines the answer we give to the question, What is a Christian? If Christianity be what the anti-supernaturalists allege, whether we call them Liberals or Modernists, it is one thing to be a Christian. But if Christianity be what we have represented it as being, it is quite another thing.

What Is a Christian?

Our answer to the question, What is a Christian? follows from our answer to the question, What is Christianity? We have defined it as *the religion that had its origin and that has its continuance in Jesus Christ, more particularly as that redemptive religion that offers salvation from the guilt of sin through His atoning death and from the corruption of sin through the regenerating and sanctifying influence of the Holy Spirit.* As a consequence, we define a Christian (1) as one who assumes a religious attitude toward Jesus Christ, and (2) as one who receives and rests upon Him for salvation from the guilt and corruption of sin. It might be supposed that some reference to the work of the Holy Spirit must needs be made in our definition of a Christian. That this is not necessary in our basic definition finds its explanation not only in the fact that it is Christ Who sends the Holy Spirit but also in the fact that the Holy Spirit never works independently of Christ, ever being content to take the things of Christ and make them clear (John 16:13-15).

A Christian, in the first place, is one who stands in a religious relation toward Jesus Christ. This means that for the Christian Jesus is more than an example of faith. It means that He is also the object of faith. Such an attitude, needless to say, is warranted only if Jesus be a supernatural being Whose rank in the scale of being is equal to that of God. Otherwise the Christian would be an idolater, one who renders to a creature the homage that belongs to God alone. It will be seen, therefore, that the Christian is not merely one who has faith in God like the faith Jesus had in God. He is rather one who has faith in Jesus Himself like that which he has in God. The anti-supernaturalist, in the nature of the case, cannot have such a faith in Jesus. And that because he is unable to see in Jesus a supernatural being of any sort, still less a supernatural being who is on an equality with the Creator of heaven and earth and all things visible and invisible. The anti-supernaturalist may see in Jesus the supreme example and guide in the field of religion. He may exhaust his vocabulary in sounding His praises as the fairest and greatest of the children of men. He may say with Renan: "Whatever be the surprises of the future Jesus will never be surpassed. His worship will grow young without ceasing, his history will provoke endless tears, his sufferings will subdue the stoutest hearts; all ages will proclaim that among the sons of men, no one has been born who is greater than Jesus." [6] He cannot, however, assume a religious attitude toward Him because that is possible only when Jesus is conceived of as God as well as man. It is true, of course, that Christians see in Jesus their example beyond compare and that they seek to imitate Him in as far as He was man and not God; but that which is

[6] *Life of Jesus,* closing paragraph.

distinctive of them in this connection is that they are worshippers of Jesus. Important as is the imitation of Jesus in the Christian religion, it is overshadowed by something more important—to wit, that Jesus is an object of worship and that Christian faith is faith in Him and only partly faith like His. No mere man, only a supernatural person—a Person Who is himself God—can be a proper object of religious worship. In harmony with this we find that neither the New Testament nor the Christian Church as a whole know anything of Christians who do not acknowledge Jesus as Lord in the fullest and richest sense the word can bear. Do we stand in a religious relation toward Jesus Christ? Do we address Him as "My Lord and my God"? If not, what intellectual right have we to call ourselves Christians?

A Christian, in the second place, is one who receives and rests upon Christ for salvation from the guilt and corruption of sin. It is not enough that we stand in a religious attitude toward Jesus Christ. Conceivably one might do that without being a Christian. Apparently the Judaizers did that—there is nothing to indicate that they did not share Paul's conception of Jesus as Lord—but Paul did not recognize them as belonging to the Christian brotherhood. For while the Judaizers acknowledged Christ as Lord they did not rest upon Him alone for their salvation. They did not commit the eternal destinies of their soul to Him without reserve. And yet one can no more be a Christian without looking to Jesus for salvation from the guilt and corruption of sin than he can be a Christian without assuming a religious attitude toward Him. There is need of insisting on this in view of the fact that recognition of the deity of Jesus is sometimes spoken of as the one distinctive mark of the Christian. It is a distinctive mark, but the recognition of Him as Saviour in the sense indicated is an equally distinctive mark.

That Christian faith is faith in Jesus, not merely faith like Jesus had, appears most clearly when we think of Him as Saviour. If our faith as Christians is merely faith like Jesus had, it must be supposed that Jesus Himself had saving faith. That would have been possible, however, only if He had been a sinner. This makes clear, as perhaps nothing else, what a dreadful misunderstanding is involved when anyone speaks of Jesus as a Christian. To speak of Jesus as a Christian is like speaking of God as a religious being. God is the prerequisite to all religion worthy of the name but He Himself is the One Being that cannot be spoken of as religious. So, in like manner, Jesus is the prerequisite to there being any Christians, and yet He is the one Person who ever dwelt upon this earth who could not Himself be a Christian. A Christian is one who receives and rests upon Jesus Christ for salvation. In the nature of the case, Jesus Himself could not do that. He could not repose trust in Himself in the sense here indicated. He was certainly, therefore, not a Christian. To allege that He was is to be blind to the difference between the Saviour and the saved. Hence Christian faith while it may be in some degree like the faith Jesus had must, first of all, be faith in Him.

A Christian, then, is one to whom Christ is both Lord and Saviour. As Lord, Jesus is the One Whom the Christian worships and obeys; as Saviour He is the One upon Whom he depends for salvation from the guilt and corruption of sin. Christ cannot be divided. He must, therefore, be taken in both of these aspects if He is to be taken at all. This means that we cannot have Christ as our Saviour without having Him at the same time as our Lord. If Christ is really our Saviour He is at the same time our Lord; and if He is our Lord we will endeavor to do as He says. "Not every one that sayeth unto me, Lord, Lord, shall enter the kingdom of heaven; but he that doeth the will of my Father who is in heaven" (Matt. 7:21). Do we stand in a religious attitude toward Jesus Christ? Do we receive and rest upon Him for salvation? Only if we can answer these questions in the affirmative have we any right to call ourselves Christians. We may be able to answer them in the affirmative without being Christians who "adorn the doctrine of God our Saviour in all things" (Titus 2:10). However, if we can answer them in the affirmative, we are Christians even though we be but "babes in Christ" whatever the number of our days. This is not to imply that we should ever be content with what we are. We should be constantly growing in grace, ever forgetting the things which are behind and reaching forth unto the things which are before, ever bringing all our thoughts and activities more and more into obedience to Christ. We should remember, moreover, that a Christian, in any adequate sense of the word, recognizes that he is a member of the body of Christ (the Church) and of the social organism. As such he is under obligation to evangelize both in the sense of endeavoring to lead others to a saving knowledge of Jesus Christ and of, as far as possible, permeating the social order with Christian principles.

It may not be out of place to add that in accomplishing his life's task the thought of reward need not be wholly absent from the Christian's thought. While it is never the controlling motive it has its place in the Christian life. Though Christians are not rewarded on account of their works, God has graciously promised to reward them in accordance with their works. We are not to suppose that all Christians are to receive the same reward. There will be differences among the redeemed. There is not going to be a dead level of uniformity in heaven any more than there is a dead level of uniformity on earth. We read in the Scriptures of those who shall be greatest and those who shall be least in the kingdom of God. We are told that just as one star differeth from another star in glory so shall it be in the resurrection of the dead. In that day, Christ will say "Well done, thou good and faithful servant" to those who have been faithful, to those who have done well, but there is no authority for saying that He will address such words of praise to those who have not done well, to those who have not been faithful.

Who Are Christians?

It is easy to answer the question, What is a Christian? once we have answered the question, What is Christianity? It is more or less impossible, however, to say whether this or that particular individual is a Christian. Here we can often only say, "The Lord knoweth them that are His" (II Tim. 2:19). No doubt we ought to be able to judge rightly of ourselves, though even here it is possible to be a Christian without being wholly assured of that fact somewhat as a man may be a legal voter while in doubt as to his legal status. In the case of others, however, it does not become us to pass anything like final judgment. The power of that faith that is specifically Christian lies in the object upon which it terminates, *viz.*, Jesus Christ. Consequently, it is the existence of such faith rather than its strength that is the essential thing. Christ, according to Christian teaching, is able to save and does save all those who put their trust in Him even though that faith be weak and wavering. While a man must have some knowledge of Christ before he can assume a religious attitude toward Him and receive and rest upon Him for salvation, it is impossible to say how much he must have. A man may have a very inadequate knowledge of Christ and still be a Christian. Even where this knowledge is extensive it is as little safe to assume that a man is a Christian because he is orthodox in his beliefs as it is to assume that he is not a Christian because he is more or less unorthodox. It is one thing to say what a Christian is, but a quite different thing to say who is and who is not a Christian.

It is sometimes asked, for instance, Can a man be a Christian who doubts or denies the virgin birth of Christ or who doubts or denies His visible personal return? It may be safely affirmed, it seems to us, that such a man is badly instructed concerning the essential doctrines of the Christian faith, but it is going too far to say that he cannot be a Christian. It is one thing to say what we must confess if we would confess the essential content of the Christian faith whole and entire. It is quite another thing to say what the terms of salvation are. The terms of salvation are simply acceptance of Christ as Lord and Saviour. If Christ is equipped to save us, and we trust Him to do this, we will be saved even if our knowledge of what it behooved Him to be and do that He might be our full and complete Saviour is inadequate or even in large degree mistaken. Logical capacity, consistency of thought, ability to comprehend the implicates of faith in Christ as Lord and Saviour, are not conditions of salvation. We are not to suppose that only the wise are saved, that weakness of intellect excludes from the kingdom of God. This is not to say that knowledge is unimportant. We must have an intelligent faith if we are to have a mature faith. It is merely to say that a saving faith may exist despite much error and ignorance. A man named Blondin walked across the cataract below Niagara Falls on a tight rope—a feat that showed that such an act is possible. A tight rope may be said to be the minimum that is needed to walk across that cataract. Most people, however, if they are to have any hope of walking across that cataract must avail themselves of the suspension bridge that spans the Niagara River at that point. So the fact that some may be saved with but little knowledge affords no warrant for supposing that the maximum of knowledge is not to be preferred. Other things being equal, we may be sure that the more adequate and the more correct our knowledge the firmer will be our faith and the more effective our service. It was because Paul knew, because he had intellectually grasped, what it behooved Christ to be and do that He might be his Lord and Saviour that he could so confidently affirm: "I know whom I have believed, and am persuaded that He is able to keep that which I have committed unto Him against that day" (II Tim. 1:12).

Evangelicals and Sacerdotalists

Subjective Christianity, as we have said, is the result of the application or appropriation of objective Christianity. We mention it afresh in order to call attention to one of the deepest lines of cleavage existing between those calling themselves Christians, *viz.,* that between Evangelicalism as it finds expression in the historic creeds of Protestantism and Sacerdotalism as it finds its fullest expression in Roman Catholicism. There is, it should not be overlooked, a large measure of agreement between Evangelicals and Sacerdotalists. Both hold that in Jesus Christ adequate provision has been made for the salvation of mankind. Both hold that subjective Christianity involves salvation from both the guilt and the corruption of sin and that ultimately Christians are to be wholly without either. They differ radically, however, concerning the method by which the benefits of Christ's work are applied to or appropriated by the individual. According to the Evangelicals God in saving men deals with them directly; according to the Sacerdotalists He deals with them indirectly through the Church which He has established as the organ through which to communicate His saving grace to men. The Church, according to the Sacerdotalists, is an external organization which, standing between the individual and God, represents Christ in His three-fold office of Prophet, Priest and King; as Prophet to teach with infallibility; as Priest to mediate Christ's saving benefits; as King to exact obedience in matters of faith and duty. While in Roman Catholicism, as in Protestantism, the ultimate object of faith is Jesus Christ, the proximate object is the Church. As a result, the temptation is ever present to its adherents to put their trust in the Church rather than in Christ Himself and to imagine that all is well with their souls for time and eternity as long as they are in good standing in the Church. What is more, it can hardly be denied that multitudes have yielded and are yielding to this temptation.

It should not be forgotten in this connection

that Roman Catholicism continues to maintain that ultimately salvation is of God and that the core of the provision God has made for the salvation of men is the atoning death of Jesus Christ. Hence from the Protestant point of view Roman Catholicism is a perversion or deformation of Christianity rather than a falsification of it as in the case of anti-supernaturalistic Liberalism or Modernism. The double confession of Evangelicalism is that salvation is of God and that God in saving men deals with them directly, not through an institution clothed with the power of God. Evangelicals, however, in opposing the interposition of the Church between the individual soul and God, should not overlook their agreement with the Sacerdotalists as over against any and all purely naturalistic conceptions of Christianity. In other words, in the zeal of their opposition to Sacerdotalism they should not overlook their deeper opposition to Naturalism. A man is not an Evangelical merely because he is not a Sacerdotalist. If the true Evangelical cannot but regard Sacerdotalism as a deformed or perverted form of Christianity, it is equally true that he cannot look upon anti-supernaturalistic Liberalism or Modernism as Christianity at all. This is not to say that there are no Christians among so-called Liberals and Modernists. Many of them are not consistently anti-supernaturalistic in their explanation of the origin and continuance of Christianity.

The Adequacy of Objective Christianity

We have pointed out that while subjective

Christianity is in constant flux, objective Christianity is a fixed reality. It remains to be added that objective Christianity is completely adequate, wholly sufficient for the purpose for which it was provided. This means that those to whom it is applied, or by whom it is appropriated, will be saved to the uttermost. This is the common belief of Christians. Calvinists and Arminians differ as to the perseverance of the saints, and Protestants and Roman Catholics differ as to purgatory, not to mention other differences, but all are agreed that those who continue to put their trust in Christ as their Saviour will ultimately be completely saved. Objective Christianity is not only a faith once for all delivered, it is a faith that will never fail those who avail themselves of its benefits.

Concretely expressed, this means that Jesus Christ is able to save and that He does completely save all those who put their trust in Him. It is the strong Son of God—to Whom all power has been committed in heaven and in earth—that Christianity proclaims. Only as Christians keep this element of power in mind can they have assurance either of their own ultimate salvation or of the ultimate triumph of the religion they profess. It constitutes one of the main elements in the good news that Christianity proclaims. Eliminate this element of power from the Christian proclamation, and it becomes a proclamation of despair rather than one of hope. For in that case the Christian proclamation as a way of life would differ from others only by reason of the greater purity and loftiness of the ideal of conduct it sets before men, and so of the greater stringency of the demands it makes upon them. Then they could but cry out that such teaching is too high for them, that they cannot attain unto it. But give this element of power its rightful place in the Christian proclamation and it retains its character as a message of hope. For then the purity and loftiness of its demands become a prophecy of that which by the help of Christ they shall one day become. What is more, they are able to proclaim it confidently and joyfully even to the worst of sinners, because they see in Jesus Christ One Who is able to break that dominion that sin has over them and to lead them on from victory to victory until that character which was actualized in Him becomes actualized in them.

The struggle for and against Christianity is not a merely intellectual struggle. It is an intellectual struggle but if it were only an intellectual struggle the Christian would have scant reason to think that Christianity will ultimately triumph—not because it occupies the less defensible position but because it must make its appeal to sinners, to those who are prejudiced against it both as a system of thought and as a way of life. As the proverb has it: "Men convinced against their will remain of the same opinion still." For their heartening and encouragement, Christians need ever to remember that while Christianity is a specific system of thought and life that calls for intellectual defense it is also a divine dynamic that energizes as only God can energize. He Who stands at its center and makes it what it is, is infinitely more than a teacher and example. He is also the Saviour of the world, the Lord and Life of humanity. It is not merely with His weak and unworthy followers that the enemies of Christianity have to reckon. They have to reckon with Jesus Himself. Since Jesus is what Christian faith declares, we may be sure that, despite all opposition, He will make His way to victory and that in the future as in the past those who seek to stay His progress will be constrained to make their own the words ascribed to Julian, the apostate, "O Galilean! Thou hast conquered!"

"For the grace of God that bringeth salvation hath appeared to all men, teaching us that denying ungodliness and worldly lusts, we should live soberly, righteously, and godly in this present world; looking for that blessed hope, and the glorious appearing of the great God and our Saviour Jesus Christ; who gave Himself for us, that He might redeem us from all iniquity, and purify unto Himself a peculiar people, zealous of good works."—TITUS 2:11-14.

Chapter VII

CHRISTIANITY AND CONDUCT

We have previously pointed out that redemption as understood by Christianity involves deliverance from the corruption as well as the guilt of sin. Salvation in the Christian sense of the word has as its goal complete sanctification and the doing of good works and good works only. Alone among ethical systems it insists upon absolute moral perfection. "Be ye therefore perfect even as your Father in heaven is perfect" is its ethical watchword. What is more, it insists on this ideal not as a limiting concept—something to be striven after but never reached—but as that which is to be realized by its genuine adherents. It is not too much to say, intellectually speaking, that no one should have anything to do with Jesus Christ who does not aspire to be ethically perfect. Such as do are concerning themselves with means fitted to bring about ends they do not desire. His name was called Jesus because He came to save His people *from* their sins. Nothing is more certain, according to Christian teaching, than that those who continue in vital relation with Jesus Christ as their Saviour will one day be morally perfect. No doubt He does not immediately save His people from the corruption of sin—as He does from the guilt of sin—but while He proceeds by process it is a process that will have that culmination. He makes the tree good that it may bear good fruit but, while this is done gradually and not without the cooperation of those in whom it takes place, yet at the end of the day it will have been done completely in the case of all who continue among His true disciples. In the meantime sincere and intelligent Christians always have before them perfection as their goal.

Some have maintained that it would have been better if Christ had not insisted on so lofty an ideal. Is it not often alleged that to set up perfection as a goal deadens effort and enthrones despair? Surely we cannot exemplify perfection. Why then strive for it? Why seek the impossible? We may agree that this ideal has never been realized on earth by any of Christ's followers and yet maintain that a man with a perfect ethical ideal will make greater progress than the man with an imperfect ethical ideal. Any lowering of our standard means a slackening of our efforts. It is ever the man with the highest ideal that is most careful to abstain from what is evil and to do what is good. Any standard that falls short of perfection permits us to look upon sin with some degree of allowance. All history and all experience support the notion that our ideal ought to be perfect no matter how imperfect may be our realization of it; and hence that Christianity exhibits practical wisdom as well as lofty aspiration when it exhorts us to take perfection as our goal. No doubt there have always been those who have alleged that the dependence that Christians place upon Christ is hostile to moral endeavor but, apart from the fact that history does not support but rather contradicts such an allegation, it should be clear to all that it is opposed to the very genius of Christianity to suppose that it can render its adherents lax as regards moral endeavor. As a religion of redemption from the corruption as well as the guilt of sin, it is to deny its nature and purpose to suppose that such is the case.

Whatever else Christianity is, it is safe to say therefore that it is an ethical movement. It has to do with the way of life, the mode of conduct, the lines along which men's activities must proceed if they would live as they ought to live. Whatever may be said to the contrary, no orthodoxy of thought, no punctilious observance of religious rites, no generosity in support of or labor in behalf of religious or philanthropic movements or organizations, will lead it to look with favor on the man whose way is otherwise the way of sin and iniquity. No matter to what part of its authoritative writings or to which of its historic creeds we may turn, we find this thought clearly and forcibly expressed. Antinomians, here and there, may have minimized the need of moral perfection, but, allowing for these few exceptions, those calling themselves Christians have always recognized not only that Christianity is an ethical movement but that we are praiseworthy Christians in proportion as its ethic finds embodiment in our daily walk and conversation. The typical Christian has always been as sensible of ethical duty as he has been exuberant with spiritual hope. The absence of any endeavor to live the sort of life Christianity commends has ever been regarded as *prima facie* evidence that those of whom this is true are not Christians. It is no doubt possible to question whether the Christian ideal of conduct is the best —we shall see that many today deny that it is— but it is not possible to deny that Christianity presents an ideal of conduct which it is mandatory for its adherents to translate into action.

It is hardly open to question that Christianity is, and in the nature of the case cannot but be, an ethical religion and as such supremely concerned about the conduct of its adherents. The drastic action taken in the case of Ananias and Sapphira can best be explained by the need of impressing upon the early Christians the fact that the religion they had embraced was through and through an ethical religion. It was of first importance that it be recognized from the start that, whatever else Christianity might be, it was a way of life, that the salvation it proclaimed was a salvation from sin not only as a blessed hope but as in some degree a present reality.

Present-Day Repudiation of Christian Ideals of Conduct

That Christianity has been from its beginning a way of life has been all but universally recognized. What is more, until rather recently it has been all but universally recognized, in Europe and America at least, that the Christian way of life is the best. Within the memory of living men even those who rejected the doctrines of Christianity together with the facts of which they are the interpretation, vied with one another in extolling the superiority of the Christian ethic. The oft quoted words of John Stuart Mill were written in 1873 and reflect what was then, and what continued for some time thereafter to be, the common view even among unbelievers. "The most valuable part of the effect on character which Christianity has produced by holding up in a divine person a standard of excellence and a model of imitation," he wrote, "is available even to the absolute unbeliever, and can never more be lost to humanity. . . . Whatever else may be taken from us by rational criticism, Christ is still left: a unique figure, not more unlike all his precursors than all his followers, even those who had the benefit of his personal preaching. . . . Religion cannot be said to have made a bad choice in pitching on this man as the ideal representative and guide of humanity; nor even yet would it be easy, even for the unbeliever, to find a better translation of the rule of virtue from the abstract into the concrete than the endeavor so to live that Christ would approve our life." [1]

The fathers of many and the grandfathers of most present-day Christians were under no necessity of defending their ethical ideals. Practically everybody admitted their superiority. This, however, is no longer the case. At the present time there is no element of the Christian faith more

[1] *Three Essays in Religion,* p. 253.

openly or more violently assailed than its ethics. One of the most outstanding characteristics of the age in which we live is the wide-spread repudiation of the Christian ideal of conduct.[2] John Neville Figgis was well within the truth when he wrote: "On all hands we hear preached a revival of Paganism. Christianity as an ethical ideal is contemned. Formerly Christians were charged with hypocrisy because they fell short of their ideal. The charge was false, although the fact was true. We do fail, fail miserably, to come up to our ideal, and we always shall, so long as it remains our ideal. Nowadays the Christian is attacked not because he fails, but in as far as he succeeds. Our Lord himself is scorned, not because he is not the revealer of love, but because he is. Hardly a single specifically Christian value is left as it was." [3]

How shall we explain this reversal of attitude toward the Christian way of life, the Christian ideal of conduct, on the part of many in America as well as Europe? Some years ago Lionel Spencer Thornton in a book entitled *Conduct and the Supernatural* ascribed it to four main causes: (1) the Rationalism of the eighteenth century, (2) the general outlook upon the world-process derived from the evolutionist theory, (3) the fatalism of the idealist philosophy of the nineteenth century, and (4) the repudiation of Christian doctrines. He rightly stressed, we think, the repudi-

[2] See pages 9-11.

[3] *The Will to Freedom*, p. 4.

ation of Christian doctrines as the most important or at least the most immediate cause of this changed attitude toward the Christian ethic. In sharp opposition to those who speak glibly and approvingly of a non-doctrinal Christianity he wrote: "The repudiation of Christian moral standards is a direct and entirely natural result of the earlier rejection of Christian dogma. No doubt far-seeing theologians foresaw all along that this would be the case; but those who repudiated the Christian creed did not themselves see it. It is indeed safe to say that they had no suspicion of it. There are still, perhaps, a few pedants who declare that the essence of Christianity is to be found in the Sermon on the Mount, and that one can be a good Christian by practicing the imitation of Christ, without taking any notice of the traditional dogmas. Such people are living in a fool's paradise; for all around them are living proofs of the fallacy of their opinions. If there is one thing that can be said with absolute certainty about this whole movement with which we are dealing, it is that the revolt is due to the previous repudiation of the doctrines upon which it is founded. The two things, belief and conduct, are indissolubly bound together; they are parts of one whole, as roots and fruit are both alike parts of one tree, organically connected." [4]

In our judgment, Thornton, in the passage just cited, placed his finger on the most important of the proximate causes of the wide-spread denial of the right of Christianity to furnish either the

[4] p. 12.

modern individual or the modern state with its moral ideals. The immediate reason why so many leading modern unbelievers like Mill and Huxley and Matthew Arnold continued to commend the Christian mode of life was that they did not realize that the Christian ideal of conduct is so tied up with Christian beliefs that the two stand or fall together. This belief runs through all of Paul's thinking and appears particularly in the fact that in nearly all his Epistles practical exhortations follow doctrinal exposition, the two being connected by what has been rightly called his "tremendous therefores." How inextricably the two are bound together in his thinking is indicated by such an individual passage as the following: "For the grace of God hath appeared, bringing salvation to all men, instructing us, to the intent that, denying ungodliness and worldly lusts, we should live soberly and righteously and godly in this present world; looking for the blessed hope and the appearing of the glory of the great God and our Saviour Jesus Christ; who gave Himself for us that He might redeem us from all iniquity and purify unto Himself a people for His own possession, zealous of good works" (Titus 2:11-14).

It seems strange that men of the intellectual acumen of those we have mentioned should not have perceived that neither the reasonableness nor the practicability of the Christian ethic can be defended except upon the assumption of the truthfulness of the doctrines of Christianity and the reality of the facts of which they are the interpretation. Nietzsche saw more clearly. He had the insight to perceive that the Christian ethic is organically connected with the Christian creed and as such inevitable if the Christian creed is true; and having rejected the Christian creed he saw that the logic of the situation demanded that he war against the Christian ideal of life.[5] And since his day it has been increasingly admitted that Nietzsche was right. It would seem, in fact, that the time is rapidly approaching when it will be generally true that those who reject the Christian creed will also reject the Christian way of life. It is hardly likely that the case of George Eliot will ever be duplicated. She rejected the basic doctrines of Christianity, was in fact virtually an atheist, and yet she defended and commended the Christian conception of conduct, however poorly she practiced it. In all probability the time is coming when non-Christians will be as unanimous in rejecting the Christian way of life as they are in rejecting the Christian creed.

In the intellectual struggle for and against the doctrines of Christianity more than the fate of the doctrines themselves is at stake. It is equally true that Christian morality is at stake. If the present attempt to uproot and throw into the discard the doctrines of Christianity should succeed, it would mean the end of our Christian culture and civilization and the supplanting of this culture and civilization by another and distinctly different type of culture and civilization. This is true because ethics are the soul of all culture. That

[5] See page 11.

which distinguishes a Christian from a non-Christian civilization, that which distinguishes non-Christian civilizations from one another, is not so much their relative developments in the arts and literature, in science and agriculture, in industry and commerce, as in the ethical ideals that pervade and control them. The chief representatives of every type of culture and civilization confess that the highest good of humanity does not consist exclusively, or even principally, in the improvement of material welfare. Even so tough-minded a materialist as Haeckel held that the kernel of culture was in the worship of the true, the beautiful and the good. It is vain therefore to suppose that our Christian culture and civilization can continue long after the moral ideals of Christianity have been repudiated.

When Christianity entered this world it found a world rich in culture and highly developed in its civilization. With that culture and civilization Christianity engaged in a life and death struggle that lasted for some three hundred years and in which at great cost and sacrifice it conquered. As a result the hegemony of the Western world passed into the hands of Christianity. For some fifteen centuries the right of Christianity to furnish both the individual and society with its moral ideal was not seriously questioned. Today, however, this right is so widely and seriously questioned that we must go back to the first three centuries of the Christian era to discover a situation similar to that which now confronts us. There were not lacking those who foresaw that the rejection of the Christian doctrines would issue in the rejection of the Christian ideals of conduct and so in the destruction of such measure of the Christian type of culture and civilization as we possessed. But most were apparently unaware that the foundations were being undermined and the fact that the Christian ideal was not openly attacked, but rather praised, no doubt acted as a smoke screen that kept them from seeing the full significance of what was taking place. Today, however, we need no special insight to perceive what confronts us. The storm clouds that have been hovering on the horizon have assumed a threatening aspect, nay more, have already begun to hurl their thunderbolts and to cast not only rain but hail upon the earth. No longer is it possible for thinking men and women to conceal from themselves the fact that the culture known as Christian is imperilled, and that we are faced with the issue whether Christianity both as a system of thought and a way of life is to be cast aside and a non-Christian conception of thought and life employed to shape the culture and civilization of the future.

The basic error of those who suppose that the ethics of Christianity are independent of its doctrines is, as we have intimated, their failure to perceive that the two are organically connected in such a sense that the one cannot live without the other. If the doctrines of Christianity are true, the ethics of Christianity are the only ethics that can justify themselves. On the other hand, if the doctrines of Christianity are false, it is impossible to vindicate either the reasonableness or the practicability of the Christian way of life. Those who think otherwise fail to realize that "the Christian religion is a unity, a supernatural way of living, based upon and inspired by supernatural facts and truths."

Let no one suppose then that zeal for Christian doctrines is a zeal for a sterile intellectualism. Far from it. We can be intelligently indifferent to Christian doctrines only as we are indifferent to Christian standards of conduct. All around us, for those who have eyes to see, there exists living proof of the fact that those who attack the Christian doctrines are at the same time attacking the Christian ethic. Nothing is more certain than that in the long run Christian doctrines and Christian morality stand or fall together. We might as well suppose that a house can stand after its foundation has been undermined or that a tree can continue to bear fruit after its roots have been cut as expect men to act like Christians when they do not think like Christians. The cry, "Christianity is life not doctrine," is folly and unbelief. In the interest of the Christian life itself it is of first importance that Christian doctrines be maintained and propagated.

We have stated that the proximate or more immediate cause of the present-day antagonism to Christian ideals of conduct is the previous repudiation of Christian doctrines—a repudiation that carries with it a denial of the facts of which the doctrines are the interpretation. Thornton directs attention to some of the more ultimate causes when he mentions the Rationalism of the eighteenth century and the evolutionism and the idealist philosophy of the nineteenth century. All these, however, have their roots in a more comprehensive and more ultimate cause, *viz.*, that naturalism of thought and sentiment which had its beginnings in the so-called "Enlightenment" of the eighteenth century and which has spread and spread until it has become an outstanding characteristic of the age in which we live. Back not only of the repudiation of the doctrines of Christianity, and of the historicity of the facts of which the doctrines are confessedly interpretations, but also of the Rationalism and evolutionism and idealistic philosophy of the eighteenth and nineteenth centuries stand the repudiation of the supernaturalism of Christianity and the adoption of a Naturalistic life and world view into which it is impossible to fit Christianity either as a system of thought or life.

The Supernatural and the Christian Way of Life

We are particularly concerned in this connection to point out that the supernatural is as essential to Christianity as a way of life as it is to Christianity as a system of thought. Here too the supernatural is the very breath of the nostrils of Christianity, not something that can be eliminated in order to make it acceptable to the present age. Here too we need only perceive the degree to which the supernatural is implicated in the ethics of Christianity to have brought home to us the fact that Christianity desupernaturalized is Christianity extinct as a way of life as well as a way of thought. Apart from the supernatural it may be possible to show that the Christian ideal of conduct is superior to all known ideals, and that this would be a more desirable world in which to live if it were more generally embraced and practiced, but, we submit, that it is not possible to show that it is practicable, and that because it requires the supernatural to make it operative. In proof of this we direct attention to the extent to which the supernatural is inextricably implicated in the Christian way of life.

1. We cannot even get started in the Christian way of life apart from the supernatural. When we first discover our whereabouts we find ourselves in the broad way that leads to death, not in the narrow way that leads to life. Moreover by the use of merely natural means—those powers that inhere in us as men—we are unable to forsake the broad way and get into the narrow way. This is not because access to the narrow way is barred, as it were, by stone walls and iron gates but because of our inability, our sheer lack of the moral strength, to leave the one and enter the other. We might as well suppose that an evil tree can produce good fruit as suppose that those corrupted by sin can by their own power set themselves in the path that leads to eternal life. Can the Ethiopian change his skin or the leopard his spots? Is it not forever true that only the good tree is able to produce good fruit while the evil tree

always and everywhere produces evil fruit? We might as well suppose that dead and decaying Lazarus of his own initiative and of his own strength could have clothed himself with the garments of youthful flesh as suppose that the sinner —who is corrupt as well as guilty—can by his own will and by his own power set his feet in the path that leadeth to moral perfection. Only as a supernatural power energizes within us is it possible for us to rise up and walk in newness of life. In other words regeneration, re-birth through the operation of the Holy Spirit, is absolutely necessary before we can get into the Christian way of life.

We are aware that a different representation is widely current. We are told rather: "The gates along the way of life stand open; whosoever will may enter in." Moreover such a representation is not employed merely to emphasize the universality of the gospel offer; it is employed to express belief in man's plenary ability to work out his own salvation. Witness the fact that we are constantly told that the Parable of the Prodigal Son contains the core of the Gospel, even the whole Gospel. We would be the last to minimize the value of this parable or to think lightly of the great truths it enshrines, but we are not blind to the fact that there is no Christ, no atonement, no Holy Spirit in it. What is the Gospel without these? If this parable contains the whole or even the core of Christianity, then, we of our own will can get up and go to God and assume the position of a child in His household whenever we choose—

no questions asked and a warm reception assured. Such a representation may be pleasing to the naturalistically minded, but, many to the contrary notwithstanding, it is not the Christian representation. In fact the extent to which it prevails in wide circles is merely an indication of the extent to which the so-called New Protestantism has departed from historic Christianity. In this connection we are especially concerned to call attention to the fact that there is no reference, direct or indirect, to the Holy Spirit in the Parable of the Prodigal Son. We are dependent on the Holy Spirit at every stage of the Christian life but our immediate concern is to stress the fact that apart from His supernatural operation in our hearts we cannot even get started in the Christian way of living. The words of Jesus are basic to Christianity as a way of life: "Verily, verily, I say unto thee, Except one be born of water and the Spirit, he cannot enter into the kingdom of God."

2. Not only can we not get started in the Christian way of life apart from the supernatural, we can make no progress in that way apart from the supernatural. It is not enough that, having gotten into the narrow way, we be told, "This is the way; walk ye in it." We need to know the rules and regulations of the road, we need adequate and dependable directions lest we lose our way. Moreover, as rational creatures we need to have motives or incentives brought to bear upon us to induce us to walk in this way rather than some other. Still

further we must have sufficient energy or power to enable us to propel ourselves along the way designated. Whether we consider the directions that have been given us, or the incentives that are brought to bear upon us, or the power that enables us to proceed along the lines desired, we are brought face to face with the fact that there is no progress in the Christian way of life apart from the supernatural.

As travelers along the Christian way of life we need directions. The directions which have been given us and which must be followed are of supernatural origin. They come to us as revealed. This means that Christianity does not regard its moral code or its ethical ideals as naturalistic in origin any more than it regards its doctrines as naturalistic in origin. If man after he had sinned had been left to himself to work out his destiny on the plane of nature he would, according to Christianity, be as ignorant of the Christian standard of conduct as he would be ignorant of the Christian doctrines. It is contrary to Christianity's own representation to suppose that the superstructure of Christian morality has been or can be erected on a naturalistic foundation. The morality of Christianity is not, according to its own claims, a man-made thing. It is a revealed morality and as such an expression of the will of God. Christianity maintains that its moral standard is objective, in the will of God rather than the will of man, and thus is something that would not exist apart from the reality and activity of the supernatural.

As travelers along this way we also need motives

or incentives. It is not enough that we have directions telling us when to turn to the right and when to the left. The question arises, Why should we proceed along the way directed? You tell me that I ought to live a Christian life. I ask, Why? There may be some other sort of life that appeals to me more strongly. And, if you are to persuade me that I ought to do as you say, you must convince me that Christianity is true, that it alone points out the path that leads to richness and fulness of life. Only on the assumption that Christianity is true is there any lasting warrant for saying that I ought to live a Christian life. But even if it be admitted that Christianity teaches the way of God in truth—an assumption that can be true only if we assume the reality and activity of the supernatural—there is need of specific motives or incentives to induce us to travel along the Christian way and, in proportion as we appreciate, come under the influence of those motives, will we speed rather than lag along the way.

We are concerned just now to point out that the main motives and incentives advanced by Christianity to induce us to proceed along the way it commends are drawn from the supernatural. Christian ethics do not disdain motives drawn from purely earthly consideration—those derived from expediency in the use of the things of this world, consideration of our fellows, love of country and such like—but its main reliance is upon motives that have no existence from the viewpoint of naturalism. We refer to those derived from God and His love. The motive drawn from the thought of rewards and punishment in a future life is also not absent from Christian ethics. But while this motive is appealed to—a motive that hangs in the air apart from the reality of a supernatural world—yet its place is near the periphery rather than the center. The central motive in the life of the Christian is represented as grateful love to the redeeming God who mercifully set His love upon us and sent His Son to die for us. "The love of Christ constraineth us; because we thus judge, that one died for all, therefore all died; and He died for all, that they that live should no longer live unto themselves, but unto Him who for their sakes died and rose again" (II Cor. 5:14-15). The grace of God as revealed in the Son of His love is the supreme motive. Its most telling exhortation is found in the appeal, "I beseech you therefore, brethren, by the mercies of God, that ye present your bodies as living sacrifices" (Rom. 12:1). No doubt we all act from mixed motives, but if this motive has no place in our lives it cannot be that we are walking in the Christian way of life. And yet only as we recognize the reality of the supernatural is there such a motive with which to reckon. When we ask why we should lead a Christian life we are always pointed to supernatural considerations. Even when purely earthly motives are also advanced, they are always advanced as subordinate to more ultimate motives drawn from the supernatural.

It is not enough, however, that we have the right directions and that we feel the urge of Christian motives. We may have the latest automobile; we may have the latest map and be certain of our route; we may be anxious to follow the route indicated; but if there is no gasoline in the tank or our ignition system is not working, we cannot advance a single mile. And so it is not enough that we know the Christian way of life and that the proper incentives be brought to bear upon us to induce us to travel in that way. Ethical teachers of all ages have bewailed the fact that "men know the good without the power to do it and that they know the evil without the power to avoid it." What we need, even more than we need instruction and incentives, is power—an energy that will enable us to realize the Christian ideal in our own lives. Apart from such power we may dream of being good in the Christian sense of the word but we will never be good. Nay, the more earnestly we strive to be good the sooner will we be driven to make our own the despairing cry to which Paul gave such striking expression: "To will is present with me, but how to perform that which is good, I find not. For the good that I would, I do not; but the evil that I would not, that I do. . . . I delight in the law after the inward man, but I see another law in my members warring against the law in my mind and bringing me into captivity to the law of sin" (Rom. 7:17-23).

On the plane of the natural the antithesis between the ideal and the attainment cannot be overcome. We must look beyond the natural if we are to regard the Christian ideal as realizable. It is because and only because Christianity looks beyond the natural to the supernatural that it has the courage to affirm that its ideal is translatable into terms of human conduct. It proclaims not only an ideal but a dynamic adequate for its realization. This dynamic is found in the supernatural Christ acting through the Holy Spirit. Apart from the living Christ, its ideal would be an unrealized and unrealizable vision. It is because and only because the Christian can do all things through Him that it is possible for the Christian to express his ideal in terms of human life and character. Apart from this element of power, Jesus would still possess significance as a moral and spiritual teacher; and yet He would differ merely in degree and not in kind from men like Socrates and Plato and Aristotle and Confucius and others. It is because of this power—a power that according to Christian teaching remains the same yesterday, today and forever—that He occupies an absolutely unique place among the moral and spiritual teachers of mankind. Others may hold before us visions of truth and duty. Jesus not only holds before us the highest of all ethical ideals, He enables us in an ever increasing measure to realize that ideal—such is Christian teaching. Surely we cannot perceive the significance of the living Christ, as envisaged by Christianity, without realizing that according to Christian teaching it is impossible to make progress along the Christian way apart from the supernatural. The power that enables men to walk along the Christian way makes clear, as perhaps no other consideration, the indispensableness of the supernatural to Christianity considered as a way of life. And herewith is given the reason why we cannot vindicate the practicability of the Christian ideal of conduct if the supernatural is denied. We may be able to show that the Christian ideal surpasses all others, and that this would be an infinitely more desirable world in which to live if it was generally embraced and lived; but, apart from the supernatural, we cannot show that it is practicable simply because it requires the supernatural to enable it to function. As well expect an automobile to run without gasoline or an electric spark as expect men to make progress in the Christian way of life apart from the living Christ or the Holy Spirit.

3. When we speak of Christianity as a way of life we imply not only that it prescribes the path along which we should go but that this path leads somewhere. If now we consider the end of the path, according to Christian teaching, we will have impressed upon us anew the futility of supposing that we can retain the Christian ethic while denying the supernatural. The Naturalist may think that he can get along without an eschatology; the Christian cannot because the goal of the road he travels lies in the world beyond. We should indeed be on our guard against supposing that Christianity regards earthly blessings as valueless, that it prizes only the world-shunning and contemplative life. The shibboleth of Christianity is not separation from the world but only from that which is evil in the world. And yet unquestionably

it finds its center of gravity in the life to come, so that it is impossible to vindicate the reasonableness of its ideal of conduct save as we recognize that supernaturalism in which alone it finds its proper setting. It is impossible to erect the superstructure of Christianity on a naturalistic foundation simply because its center of gravity lies in a supernatural world. If such an attempt is made, the superstructure conceived is such as would inevitably topple over of its own weight. On the assumption—the assumption of naturalism—that there is no such supernatural reality as the God and Father of our Lord and Saviour Jesus Christ, and that the present economy is but a short span of life between two eternities of death, it is altogether certain that the Christian ethic does not indicate the kind of men we need to be or the lines along which our activities may most profitably proceed.

We have been concerned to make clear that it is impossible to vindicate either the reasonableness or the practicability of the Christian ethic apart from the supernatural. This is true because the supernatural is as indispensable to Christianity considered as a way of life as it is to Christianity considered as a system of thought. Eliminate the supernatural and Christianity is no longer tenable either as a system of thought or a way of life. Those who suppose that they can keep Christianity as a way of life while rejecting it as a system of thought overlook the fact that the two are organically connected in such a way that the death of the one inevitably means the death of the other. This may not appear immediately as evidenced by the fact that writers like Mill and Huxley and Matthew Arnold and George Eliot continued to extol the superiority of the Christian ethic after they had rejected the facts and doctrines with which for good or evil it is inextricably bound. It is equally true, however, that the fact that a tree is destined to die does not appear immediately after its roots have been cut. Its death, none the less, does inevitably result. And so it is as regards the Christian ethic after its roots in Christian doctrine have been cut. Men like Mill and Huxley and Arnold are inevitably followed by men like Nietzsche and Freud and Shaw who are as outspoken in rejecting the morals of Christianity as they are in rejecting its doctrines. There is nothing surprising therefore in the present-day revolt against Christian moral standards, it is only what was to be expected as soon as there was anything like a wide-spread rejection of Christian doctrines. It is vain to expect a general return to the half-way position of men like Mill and Huxley—the position held by so many of the generation immediately preceding us. What may be expected is that more and more those who reject the creed of Christianity will also reject its standards of moral conduct. Only where the distinctive doctrines of Christianity are restored to honor and acceptance because true, can we have any well-grounded hope that there will be a general acceptance of Christian ideals. If this cannot be done, and inasfar as it cannot be done, it is futile to suppose that the culture and civilization of the future will be dominated by Christian ideals of character and conduct.

We have been even more concerned, however, to make clear that Christianity is through and through an ethical religion, that it utterly fails of its purpose inasfar as it does not produce good men who will perform good works. There is no more serious heresy than the heresy of antinomianism. Such a heresy denies the very end for which Christianity exists. "He gave Himself for us that He might redeem us from all iniquity and purify unto Himself a people for His own possession, zealous of good works." Christianity is not a redemptive religion in the Biblical sense of the word unless it includes right conduct.

"The Scripture cannot be broken."—JOHN 10:35.

"All Scripture is given by inspiration of God, and is profitable for doctrine, for reproof, for correction, for instruction in righteousness: that the man of God may be perfect, thoroughly furnished unto all good works."—II TIM. 3:16.

Chapter VIII

CHRISTIANITY AND THE BIBLE

Christians have always had a Bible. From the beginning they accepted the Old Testament as an authoritative rule of faith and practice. They have not, however, always had a New Testament inasmuch as its earliest books were not written until some twenty years after the death of Christ while the latest were not written until some sixty years thereafter. Obviously, then, there was a period during which Christianity was largely dependent upon oral teaching rather than written records. It is conceivable, therefore, that Christianity could have gotten along without a New Testament. There is small reason to think, however, that Christian teaching would have been preserved with any degree of purity and integrity if it had not been given fixedness and durability by being put into written form. From the fact that Christianity made marked progress while the Apostles and their immediate followers were still living, it by no means follows that the New Testament was not practically if not absolutely necessary for its continued well being.

A comparison of the apostolic and the post-apostolic writers apprises us of what, humanly speaking, would have happened to Christian teaching if it had not been given written form in the apostolic age. In the history of Christian thought, there is perhaps no gulf so great as that which divides the apostolic age from the age immediately succeeding. Continuity is evident but at such a lower level that had Christianity been dependent upon the men of the early post-apostolic age to transmit it to those who should come after them, there is every reason to think, humanly speaking, that the movement would long ago have run into the sand.

When the New Testament, along with the Old Testament, was all but lost during the Middle Ages Christian faith suffered a tragic eclipse. It was Luther's discovery of the Bible that led to the Reformation. Suppose there had been no Bible to discover, what reason is there to think that Christianity would have taken on new life at that time? Such considerations as these advise us of what might possibly have happened if there had been no New Testament. Emil Brunner is well within the truth when he says: "Christian faith is faith in the Bible. . . . That which holds together all the Churches of the world, from Roman Catholicism to the Quakers, from Luther to Cardinal Newman, that which throughout all historical changes of the Church has remained the same, the source from which Christianity has again and again drawn the power of renewal, is the Bible. During the nineteen hundred years of its history the Church has been more than once sick unto death; two hundred years ago Voltaire prophesied its end as certain in the near future. In the very house in which he made that prophecy there is at present an office of the British Bible Society, which annually sends out millions of Bibles in all languages into the world. It is the Bible which has again and again made the Church young and sound. True, there would be no Bible without the Church, but it is just as true that there would be no Church without the Bible. Christianity without the Bible would long ago have degenerated into an unrecognizable caricature. When we say that Christian faith is belief in Jesus Christ, we tacitly imply that it is faith in the Bible. No Bible—no Christ; no Bible—no Word of God." [1]

Brunner from whom we have just quoted does not, as we shall see, identify the words of the Bible with the Word of God and so repudiates the belief that the Bible is infallible. We should agree with him to the extent at least of admitting that this belief is not essential to the existence of Christianity. In the history of the Christian Church there has perhaps been no more outstanding champion of the infallibility of the Bible than the late Professor B. B. Warfield and yet he says: "I am far from contending that without such an inspiration there could have been no Christianity. Without any inspiration we could have had Christianity; yea, and men could still have heard the truth, and through it been awakened, and justified, and sanctified and glorified. The verities of our faith would remain historically proven true to us—so

[1] *The Word and the World* (Charles Scribner's Sons), p. 82.

bountiful has God been in his fostering care—even had we no Bible; and through these verities salvation." [2]

The Church Doctrine

It is one thing, however, to deny that Christianity stands or falls according as the Bible is fallible or infallible but quite another thing to admit that as a matter of fact the Bible we have is a fallible Bible. Whether the Bible be fallible or infallible, the immemorial doctrine of the Church has been that it is infallible. This view finds expression in all the great creeds of the Church—Greek Catholic, Roman Catholic and Protestant. Catholics and Protestants differ, it is true, on such important questions as the perspicuity and the sufficiency of Scripture—the former denying and the latter affirming that the ordinary lay-member of the Church is qualified to interpret the Scriptures for himself—but on the question whether the written Word is wholly trustworthy in all its statements—factual, doctrinal and ethical—they are in essential harmony.

It is frequently alleged that Luther and Calvin did not hold the view of the Bible expressed, for instance, in the Westminster Standards. As to Calvin there is not even plausible ground for denying that he received the Bible in all its parts as the Word of God. Somewhat greater plausibility attaches to the claim that Luther held a lax view of inspiration because he did not place James, Jude, Hebrews and the Apocalypse on the same level

[2] *The Inspiration and Authority of the Bible* (The Pres. and Ref. Pub. Co.), pp. 210-211.

with the other New Testament books but to see in this evidence that he did not believe in the infallibility of Scripture is to overlook the fact that he did not regard these books as parts of genuine Scripture—looked upon them in fact somewhat as Protestants in general look upon the Apocrypha. But while he differed from the common view as regards the *extent* of Scripture he did not differ from it as regards the *nature* of Scripture. Such books as he accepted as Scripture—all of the Old Testament and all of the New Testament but the four books mentioned—were to him the very Word of God.[3]

It is not open to reasonable doubt—and is doubted by few—that it was the general belief of those calling themselves Christians, previous to the eighteenth century, that the Bible is the Word of God and as such fully trustworthy. All, it is true, did not share this view of the Bible. For instance, the Socinians, the predecessors of our modern Unitarians, had originated and certain Arminians had adopted the view that the inspiration of the Bible is confined to matters of faith and practice. In recent years it has been alleged that this view was incorporated in the Westminster Confession of Faith where after citing the books of the Old and New Testaments it adds: "All of which are given by inspiration of God, to be the rule of faith and life" (Chap. 1, sec. 2). This allegation, however, lacks both exegetical and historical support. This statement was placed in the Confes-

[3] See *Luther and the Scriptures* (The Wartburg Press), by Dr. M. Rue.

sion, not as a definition of inspiration but rather as part of its definition of Scripture. It is Scripture, not inspiration, that this statement was employed to define. What the Confession affirms is that all the books of the Bible, since they are inspired, are "the rule of faith and practice." What is more, this view did not find for itself a place among British theologians until the publication in 1690 of the "Five Letters Concerning the Inspiration of the Holy Scriptures," taken from Le Clerc and translated out of the French, *i.e.*, after the completion of the Westminster Standards. Had the Westminster Divines been sympathetic to this view, it is altogether certain that they would not have asserted that "all the books of the Old and New Testaments" are "the Word of God written," that they have "God (who is truth itself)" for their "author," that in the originals they are "immediately inspired by God" and so of "infallible truth and divine authority," and that "a Christian believeth to be true, whatsoever is revealed in the Word, for the authority of God himself speaking therein."

Views of the Bible

But while previous to the so-called Enlightenment of the eighteenth century it was all but universally held by those calling themselves Christians that the Bible is the Word of God in such a sense that whatever it says God says, the situation that confronts us today is very different. In proportion as the naturalistic view, which professes to explain the whole world, including religion, without recourse to any supernatural factor, has gained ground, what may rightly be called the church-doctrine of inspiration has been, as was to be expected, increasingly thrown into the discard. Where this view has been whole-heartedly adopted the church-doctrine has been rejected *in toto* and its opposite openly proclaimed, *viz.*, that the Bible like all other books is the word of man. Most of those calling themselves Christians have not gone that far but many of them have been more or less influenced by the current naturalism. As a result we have a number of views that mediate between the notion that the Bible is the Word of God and the notion that it is the word of man. The various views of the Bible commended today may with substantial accuracy be subsumed under the following four heads:

1. There is the view of those whose watchword is, *the Bible is the Word of God.* This view does not overlook the fact that the Bible was written by human hands and that the individuality of its several writers is everywhere obvious. It is mere caricature of this view to represent it as implying that the Biblical writers were little more than stenographers and to dub its theory of inspiration the "dictation" theory. No doubt it is frequently asserted that the Bible cannot be a human book and at the same time the very Word of God on the ground that the limitations of the human writers cannot but extend to their writings. Such a notion is, to say the least, inadequately theistic. It assumes that men exist, to some degree at least,

wholly independent of God and that when God wanted to make known to men His will for their salvation He was under the necessity of looking down upon the earth and seeking among its denizens those who, on the whole, were best suited to His purpose, when as a matter of fact God was fully able by providence and grace to prepare the men needed to achieve His purpose in such a way that they would be perfectly equipped for the task assigned them. We are told, writes Warfield, that "as light that passes through the colored glass of a cathedral window is light from heaven, but is stained by the tints of the glass through which it passes; so any word of God which is passed through the mind and soul of a man must come out discolored by the personality through which it is given, and just to that degree ceases to be the pure word of God." "But," he pertinently asks, "what if this personality has itself been formed by God into precisely the personality it is, for the express purpose of communicating to the word given through it just the coloring which it gives it? What if the colors of the stained-glass window have been designed by the architect for the express purpose of giving to the light that floods the cathedral precisely the tone and quality it receives from them? What if the word of God that comes to His people is framed by God into the word of God it is, precisely by means of the qualities of the men, formed by Him for the purpose, through which it is given?" [4] To deny that God is capable of doing this and to affirm that in the nature of

[4] *Biblical and Theological Studies* (The Pres. and Ref. Pub. Co.), pp. 155-156.

the case the Bible cannot be the pure Word of God because given through human instrumentality is to assume a non-theistic or at least an inadequately theistic view of reality.

2. In the second place there is the view that *the Bible is the word of man*. This is necessarily the view of all thorough-going Naturalists whether of the materialistic or pantheistic type. If there is no God, or if such God as is recognized comes to consciousness only in man, obviously there can be no word of God in distinction from the word of man. Whatever value, therefore, these may ascribe to the Bible they cannot regard it as other than the word of man. It is not only the out-and-out Naturalists, however, whose view of the Bible is to be subsumed under this head. There are supernaturalists also, supernaturalists moreover who are widely recognized as Christian leaders, for whom the Bible is the word of man and no more. We have in mind particularly those who hold that revelation is by deed but not by word. Many of these attach a high value to the Bible. They hold that in the Bible is found the record of the great deeds that God has wrought for the salvation of men but they claim that He has left it to men to report and interpret those deeds. They quote with approval the statement: "The Bible is not so much the inspired record of history as the record of an inspired history." It is essentially the view of Dr. C. C. Morrison in "What is Christianity?" in which while stressing the fact that Christianity is an historical (though not

supernatural) religion he claims that its doctrines are "human constructs." "The entire body of concepts or ideas, whether biblical, creedal, or experiential, which enter into Christianity, constitute the human ideology of the Christian community, and should be treated as such, and not as divine revelation."[5] Some of those who take this view of the Bible are more in harmony with historical Christianity than others but according to all alike, the Bible contains but a human record of whatever facts may lie at the basis of Christianity while whatever interpretations the Bible may contain of these facts are the result of human reflection on them. This means of course that the Bible may be mistaken both in its record of facts and in its interpretation of them.

3. In the third place there is the view that *the Bible contains the Word of God.* This is the view that has been most widely accepted by those claiming to be Christians who have held lax views of the inspiration of the Bible. Some of these have held that the Bible is inspired only in *matters of faith and practice,* others that it is inspired only as it reports the *mysteries* of the faith (matters undiscoverable by man), still others that it is inspired as regards its *thoughts or ideas* but not as regards its words. In all its forms, however, it holds that the Bible is inspired only in part and that its readers are under the necessity of discriminating between what is the Word of God and what is the word of man. Needless to say some holding

[5] p. 170.

this view find much more of the Word of God in the Bible than do others. Advocates of this view range all the way from men like James Orr and James Denney—men whose attitude toward the Bible and the teaching they derived therefrom approximated to that of those who say that the Bible is the Word of God—to the Socinians, among whom the view seems to have originated, and their present-day Unitarian successors. All who hold this view find in the Bible more or less that they regard as the word of man.

4. In the fourth place there is the view that *the Bible becomes the Word of God*. While this view had its forerunners in such a dictate as that of Coleridge, to the effect that the test of the Word of God in the Bible is whether it "finds" us, it is only since the rise of the Dialectical Theology of Barth and Brunner that it has become widespread. According to these men the Word of God is within the Bible but in it only potentially. They never identify the Word of God and the Bible—both hold decidedly radical critical views of the Bible and both flatly reject anything like verbal inspiration—yet they hold that the Word of God within the Bible may at any time become to its readers the Word of God; or rather that some part of the Word of God within the Bible may, inasmuch as they hold that the whole of the Word of God within the Bible is never to any individual the Word of God at one and the same time—rather that only a small part of it is, now one part and now another. According to Barth and Brunner,

the Bible becomes to us the Word of God only as God speaks to us directly from it. The Word of God is never an objective statement, something to which we can point and say, That is the Word of God. It always consists of a direct address to the individual soul. God is always the subject, never the object of the address. It is always a case of God speaking to some particular man. "The Bible," says Barth, "is God's Word, so far as God speaks through it." To cite Berkhof: "The Word of God (according to the Barthians) can never become static, can never be so objectified that we can lay our hands on it and say, Here it is. It does not lie in a book as an abiding possession of man, of which he can make use. It is always God speaking to, God addressing man, that is, some particular man. . . . Strictly speaking, it cannot even be said that parts of the Bible are in themselves the Word of God—for this would again make the Word static—but parts of it may become for some individual the Word of God, and then come to that individual with the force of a personal message." [6] It will be seen, therefore, that while this view of the Bible resembles somewhat the view that the Bible *contains* the Word of God, it should nevertheless be rather sharply distinguished from it. The Barthians reject this view as no less static than the view that says the Bible *is* the Word of God. Yet the Barthians do not hesitate to employ the words "the Bible is the Word of God" because they hold not merely that some parts but that

[6] *The Word of God and the Reformed Faith* (Baker's Book House), p. 69.

all parts of the Bible, despite its historical, scientific and other inaccuracies, may become to its readers the very Word of God since God may at any time speak to them through the words of the Bible.

We have called attention to the various views of the Bible held today. In as far as these views are anti-supernaturalistic in character they involve the denial of Christianity rightly so called inasmuch as the supernatural is of the very essence of such Christianity. However, in as far as that is not the case, they do not necessarily involve its complete rejection. They may, at the worst, only involve a reduced or truncated Christianity. Hence, however much we may deplore these lowered views of the trustworthiness of the Bible we should not go to the extreme of denying the name of Christian to all who advocate them. However essential to the well-being of Christianity we may regard the entire trustworthiness of the Bible as a record and interpretation of the redemptive deeds of God, we should not go to the extreme of asserting that Christianity stands or falls with such belief. Here we avail ourselves of the words of the late Dr. J. Gresham Machen whom no one will accuse of having held any of the lowered views of inspiration referred to. In *Christianity and Liberalism* he wrote:

"It must be admitted that there are many Christians who do not accept the doctrine of plenary inspiration. That doctrine is denied not only by the liberal opponents of Christianity, but also by many true Christian men. There are many Christian men in the modern Church who find in the origin of Christianity no mere product of evolution but a real entrance of the creative power of God, who depend for their salvation, not at all upon their own efforts to lead the Christ life, but upon the atoning blood of Christ—there are many men in the modern Church who thus accept the central message of the Bible and yet believe that the message has come to us merely on the authority of trustworthy witnesses unaided in their literary work by the supernatural guidance of the Spirit of God. There are many who believe that the Bible is right at the central point, in its account of the redeeming work of Christ, and yet believe that it contains many errors. Such men are not really liberals, but Christians; because they have accepted as true the message upon which Christianity depends. A great gulf separates them from those who reject the supernatural act of God with which Christianity stands or falls." [7]

The Self-Testimony of the Bible

It is frequently said that the doctrine of the plenary inspiration of Scripture is based upon an *a apriori* assumption of what the Bible should be, not upon what the Bible actually is. Such is not the case. It is based on the exegetical fact that this is the doctrine taught in the Bible itself. It is this that accounts for both the origin and the persistence of this doctrine. It is the Church doctrine

[7] p. 75.

but, before it was the Church doctrine, it was the Bible doctrine. This testimony of the Bible to its own trustworthiness, though one of the clearest phenomena of Scripture, and of the utmost practical importance in accounting for the origin and continued persistence of the Church doctrine of the Bible, is persistently ignored or denied by many of those who impugn the full trustworthiness of the Bible.

Were it not for the fact that the Bible bears witness to its own full trustworthiness it seems clear that no one would be justified in dogmatically affirming that it is without error. The most that any one could possibly say in that case would be that the Bible contains no proved errors, seeing that even the most erudite of scholars lacks the knowledge that would warrant him in asserting that a book written so many centuries ago and dealing with so many matters, in so many periods of history, is without error. The case is quite different, however, in view of the Bible's own witness. Because of that it is possible to affirm its inerrancy without possessing superhuman knowledge. If the Bible contains no proved errors—a truly amazing fact, if fact it is—it is possible to assert that the Bible is without error without proving a universal negative. In that case our confidence in its writers may be such that we will be warranted in accepting statements made by them as true that we have no means of verifying somewhat as our confidence in the trustworthiness of a friend may be such that we will accept without question statements made by him that we have no means of verifying.

The practical importance of this self-testimony of the Bible is further evidenced by the fact that the conclusion at which students of the Bible arrive concerning the trustworthiness of the Bible is found to hinge largely on the degree of recognition they give to this phenomenon. If we ignore or deny this self-testimony, we are shut up to an inductive study of the evidence. However, by the use of the inductive method alone the most we can possibly affirm is that the Bible is free of proved errors. If however we give due recognition to this self-testimony as itself a phenomenon of the Bible, we will be led to see the wisdom of first of all ascertaining what the Scriptures teach as to their own trustworthiness and then of searching them to see whether the other phenomena of Scripture accord with that teaching. If there are phenomena in Scripture that are clearly and indubitably out of accord with the Bible's own teaching as to its inspiration, then so much the worse for that teaching; but let us not overlook the fact that unless there are phenomena that clearly and indubitably contradict that teaching, they are merely difficulties in the way of accepting it—not disproof of it. It takes *proved errors,* not merely *difficulties,* to demonstrate that the self-witness of the Bible is false. This point is so important that we add Dr. Warfield's statement: "If we start from the Scripture doctrine of inspiration, we approach the phenomena with the question whether they will negative this doctrine, and we find none able to stand against it, commended to us as true, as it is, by the vast mass of evidence that is available to prove the trustworthiness of the Scriptural writers as teachers of doctrine. But if we start simply with a collection of the phenomena, classifying and reasoning from them, whether alone or in conjunction with the Scriptural statements, it may easily happen with us, as it happened to certain of old, that meeting with some things hard to be understood, we may be ignorant and unstable enough to wrest them to our own intellectual destruction, and so approach the Biblical doctrine set upon explaining it away. The value of having the Scripture doctrine in our hands is thus fairly illustrated by the ineradicable inability of the whole negative school to distinguish between *difficulties* and *proved errors*.

"If, then, we ask, what are we to do with the numerous phenomena of Scripture inconsistent with verbal inspiration, which, so it is alleged, 'criticism' has brought to light, we reply: Challenge them in the name of the New Testament doctrine, and ask for their credentials. They have no credentials that can stand before that challenge. No single error has yet been demonstrated to occur in Scripture as given by God to His Church. And every critical student knows that the progress of investigation has been a continuous process of removing difficulties, until scarcely a shred of the old list of 'Biblical errors' remains to hide the nakedness of this moribund contention.

"To say that we do not wish to make claims 'for which we have only this to urge that they cannot be absolutely disproved' is not to the point; what is to the point is to say that we cannot set aside the presumption arising from the general trustworthiness of Scripture that its doctrine of inspiration is true, by any array of contradictory facts, each one of which is fairly disputable. We must have indisputable errors—which are not forthcoming." [8]

In the immediately preceding paragraphs we have taken for granted that the Bible bears clear witness to its own trustworthiness, that it comes to us claiming to be the Word of God and as such authoritative in all its teachings. In view of the pivotal importance of this claim it seems advisable to show that the Bible actually makes this claim.

The testimony of the Bible to its own trustworthiness is most abundant with reference to the Old Testament. This, of course, finds its explanation in the fact that the entire Scripture of the Old Testament was already in existence before any of the books of the New Testament were written. In interpreting the testimony of the New Testament to the Old Testament it is highly important to keep in mind contemporary Jewish thought concerning the Old Testament Scriptures. The New Testament itself makes clear that the Jews held the Old Testament in utter reverence. Apart from the New Testament we have explicit

[8] *The Inspiration and Authority of the Bible* (The Pres. and Ref. Pub. Co.), pp. 225-226.

statements by men like Philo and Josephus to the same effect. According to the Talmud, as cited by the *Encyclopaedia Biblica* (p. 4330) and other authorities, the denial of the heavenly origin of the Torah made a man an apostate and excluded him from the future age. Among the Jews three things were esteemed as peculiarly sacred: the Temple, the Sabbath, and the Scriptures. They found fault with the attitude of Jesus and His disciples toward the Temple and the Sabbath; but there is nothing to indicate that they took any exception to their attitude toward the Scriptures. Had either Jesus or His disciples uttered a single word against the Old Testament we may be sure that the reaction of the ever-watchful Jews would have been no less hostile than swift. The only possible explanation of their failure to find fault with Jesus and His disciples at this point is that they, like the Jews themselves, taught that the Scriptures are completely trustworthy.

It is quite true that some have alleged that Jesus in the Sermon on the Mount criticised the Old Testament as faulty. This, however, is easily refuted. Throughout Matt. 5:21-48 the contrast is not between Jesus' own teachings and the Old Testament but between Jesus' interpretation of the Old Testament and that of the Jews. Ordinarily when Jesus quotes the Old Testament He employs the formula, "It is written" or its equivalent but here He uses the formula, "Ye have heard that it was said," thereby indicating that He had in mind traditional interpretations of the

Old Testament rather than its actual teachings.[9] It is hardly open to denial that in all four of the Gospels Jesus is pictured as believing the Old Testament to be the infallible Word of God. The finality of His "It is written" in Matthew 4:4, 7, 10 and elsewhere, together with such dicta as "Ye do err not knowing the Scripture" (Matt. 22:29) and "The Scripture cannot be broken" (John 10:35) make clear that He looked on the Old Testament as authoritative in all its parts. Since Jesus is represented in all four of the Gospels as believing in the divine trustworthiness of the Old Testament, it is as obvious that their authors—Matthew, Mark, Luke and John—must all have shared that belief as it is inconceivable that these men, His ignorant and untutored disciples, should have ascribed to Him a view of the Old Testament they themselves did not hold.

Paul and Peter add their testimony. In II Timothy 3:16, Paul tells us that "All Scripture given by inspiration of God is profitable" or "Every Scripture inspired of God is also profitable." It makes comparatively little difference whether we accept the translation of the Authorized or the Revised Version. In either case what is affirmed is affirmed of the "Holy Scriptures" or "Sacred Writings" of the preceding verse. It is important, however, to note that the word translated "given by inspiration of God" or "inspired of God"

9 See the chapter on "The Authority of the Old Testament and the Authority of Christ" in *The Witness of Matthew and Mark to Jesus* by Professor Ned B. Stonehouse.

means literally "God-breathed" and hence that it ascribes a supernatural origin to the written Scriptures, not merely certain profitable functions.[10] No doubt if this passage stood alone in Paul's writings it would be possible to maintain that it does not necessarily mean that the Old Testament is wholly free of error; but when we consider that for him "Scripture says" is equivalent to saying "God says" (Gal. 3:8; Rom. 9:17) it cannot be even plausibly denied that Paul offers clear testimony to the complete trustworthiness of Scripture. The testimony of Peter is to the same effect. In II Peter 1:19-21, he affirms that every prophecy of Scripture affords a sure ground of confidence because "no prophecy ever came by the will of man; but men spake from God being moved by the Holy Spirit." It is questionable whether in this particular passage "every prophecy of Scripture" means the Old Testament as a whole or only the portion that is specifically prophetic, but at any rate it asserts that large portions of it are of divine origin and as such trustworthy.

The testimony thus far adduced has to do only with the Old Testament. Apart from the fact that few, if any, calling themselves Christians ascribe an infallibility to the Old Testament that they deny the New Testament, it is clear that the New Testament writers themselves extend the concep-

10 This was fully proven by Dr. B. B. Warfield in the article "God-Inspired Scripture" in the *Presbyterian and Reformed Review*, January 1900 (reprinted in *The Inspiration and Authority of the Bible*, pp. 295-296), as Dr. James Moffatt conceded in *The Approach to the New Testament*, p. 72.

tion of "Holy Scripture" to include their own writings (I Cor. 14:37; II Thess. 3:14; II Peter 3:15-16). Moreover, the evidence is clear that the early Christians placed the books of the New Testament on a par with those of the Old from the very beginning. Not only does Peter in his Second Epistle (3:16) put the Epistles of Paul on a level with the "other Scriptures," *i.e.*, the Old Testament, and not only does Paul in I Tim. 5:18 quote from Deuteronomy and Luke under the common head of "Scripture," but the same is done in the earliest post-apostolic Christian literature. Polycarp in 115 A.D. unites the Psalms and Ephesians in exactly the same way and a short time thereafter Clement unites Isaiah and Matthew in the same way. Some period elapsed before all the churches possessed all the books of the New Testament but as soon as they were received and recognized as duly authenticated parts of Scripture they were treated with the same deference as the Old Testament. The significance of this for the New Testament is very great. In view of the high estimate the early Christians attached to the Old Testament it is inconceivable that they should from the very beginning have attached a similar estimate to the books of the New Testament if they were not persuaded that they also had been written under the influence of the Holy Spirit. From the first, apostolicity was the test of canonicity—not necessarily in the sense of apostolic authorship but in the sense of apostolic content and authority. It was uncertainty as to their apostolicity in this sense that accounts for the slowness with which some of the churches came to accept Hebrews, James, Revelation and some of the lesser so-called Catholic Epistles as genuine parts of Holy Scripture. However, they accepted them as such as soon as they were convinced of this.

Is This Self-Testimony True?

We have directed attention to some of the testimony that the Scriptures offer as to their character. Enough has been cited to make clear that there is this difference between the fossils which the geologists investigate and the Scriptures—the fossils do not speak for themselves but the Scriptures do. There is no warrant for ignoring this testimony. It may prove to be false but it should no more be ignored than the testimony of a defendant in court should be ignored. In fact, it so manifestly provides the common sense starting point for an inductive study of the facts of Scripture that the plain man is apt to suppose that the mere fact that many discuss the trustworthiness of the Scriptures with no reference to it is an indication that the Bible contains no such testimony. But granting that the testimony exists, is it true? Do the contents of Scripture as a whole contradict it? Certainly there is no want of voices telling us that such is the case. The testimony, even if it be avowedly the testimony of Christ and His Apostles, cannot be accepted if it is contradicted by plain facts. The last thing Christ would have us do is to confess as true what we know to be false. Did not He Himself say, "To this end have I been born, and to this end am I come into the world, that I might bear witness unto the truth?" (John 18:37). The poorest possible definition of faith is that which defines it as "believing what we know ain't so." We must at least have a faith we believe to be true. Let this testimony, even the testimony of Christ Himself, be tested by the facts wherever learned, and let the test be all the more stringent because of the issues involved, but at the same time let us be on our guard against rejecting this testimony because of counter-testimony which cannot itself bear cross-examination.

No one denies that an examination of the other phenomena of Scripture reveals that which is apparently out of harmony with the claim the Bible makes for itself. It is one thing, however, we repeat, to find difficulties and quite another thing to find proved errors. Our creed will indeed be a short one if it contains only those articles against which no serious objections can be urged. There is not an article in the Apostles' Creed against which plausible objections are not urged. Even its primary assertion, "I believe in God the Father Almighty, Maker of heaven and earth," is widely rejected and that by men of learning and ability. What boots it, then, that difficulties stand in the way of accepting the Scriptural testimony, seeing that there is not a single doctrine distinctive of Christianity that is not held despite difficulties? If, however, not only difficulties but proved errors confront us when we examine the Scriptures, it is evident that the Bible bears false witness concerning itself. We are aware, of course, that many proved errors—in science, philosophy, history and morals—are openly predicated of the Scriptures. We believe, however, that their number shrinks almost to the vanishing point when due weight is given the following considerations.

1. It is one thing to say that the Scriptures contain statements out of harmony with the teachings of modern science and philosophy, but a distinctly different thing to say that they contain proved errors. Strictly speaking there is no modern science and philosophy but only modern scientists and philosophers—who differ endlessly among themselves. It is only on the assumption that the discordant voices of present-day scientists and philosophers are to be identified with the voice of Science and Philosophy that we are warranted in saying that the Bible contains errors because its teachings differ from those of these scientists and philosophers. Does anyone really believe that Science and Philosophy have now reached, even approximately, their final form? Is it not nearer the truth to say that they are so far from having reached their final form that, if the teachings of the Bible were in complete harmony with present-day science and philosophy, it is altogether certain that they will be out of harmony with the science and philosophy of the future? If, for example, the anti-supernaturalism of so much of the science and philosophy of today is to be characteristic of Science and Philosophy when they have reached their final forms, then, unquestionably the Bible contains many proved errors. Who, however, is competent to assert that such will be the case?

But unless it be certain that the science and philosophy of the future will be essentially one with the science and philosophy current today, we obviously go beyond the evidence when we affirm that the Bible contains proved errors on the ground that its teachings are out of harmony with the teachings of present-day scientists and philosophers.

2. It is frequently and confidently charged that the Scriptures contain errors on the ground that they contain moral teachings out of harmony with good ethics. One of the outstanding characteristics of the present age, as we have previously pointed out, is its wide-spread repudiation of the Christian standard of conduct. It ought to be clear to all that it is one thing to say that the Bible contains moral teachings that do not harmonize with those of Nietzsche and G. B. Shaw and H. G. Wells and Bertrand Russell and saying that it contains moral teachings that are actually wrong. We can freely admit the former while flatly denying the latter. This is not to assert that there are no serious moral difficulties in the way of believing in the complete trustworthiness of Scripture. Many of these moral difficulties, however, have no deeper root than the failure to recognize the progressiveness of revelation within the limits of the historical period covered by Scripture. Here too there is "first the blade, then the ear, after that the full corn in the ear." Others have no deeper root than the failure to distinguish between what the Scriptures record and what they sanc-

tion. Those whose roots strike deepest have to do with such matters as the destruction of the Canaanites, the Imprecatory Psalms, the substitutionary atonement, and the teaching of everlasting punishment. Even when rightly interpreted the Scriptural representations in regard to these and similar matters raise difficulties that are widely felt to be extremely serious. It should be noted, however, that these representations are morally wrong only on the assumption that there is not, or at least ought not to be, any such thing as retributive justice. It is because of the wide-spread denial of retributive justice as an attribute of God that so many regard these representations of Scripture as unworthy and immoral. Since the World Wars and their awful accompaniments there is less disposition to condemn such conceptions of justice as sub-Christian and even worse. Be that as it may, throughout the Scriptures, in the teachings of Christ as well as in those of Prophets and Apostles, God is represented as holy and righteous as well as loving, and only those who revolt at the idea of retributive justice will suppose that the approval the Scriptures give of God's punishment of the wicked affords any warrant for affirming that the Bible contains errors.

3. The Scriptures are often said to contain proved errors because they contain statements and representations out of harmony with the "assured results" of modern Biblical criticism. This is to ignore the fact that there is criticism and criticism. As a matter of fact there are no "assured results"

that are accepted by all critical scholars. There are not lacking scholars of the highest standing who hold that literary and historical criticism leaves the trustworthiness of the Bible unimpaired. There is nothing strange, of course, in the fact that certain scholars should attach such weight to the validity of their own critical methods and the soundness of their own critical conclusions as to assert that the Bible contains errors if it contains anything that does not accord with what seems to them "assured results." It is open to others, however, to believe that better critical methods and more ability to draw sound conclusions would have brought them to a different set of "assured results." If the Graf-Wellhausen-Driver-Pfeiffer view of the Old Testament, for example, is the true view, the Bible unquestionably contains many proved errors. Their reconstruction of the Old Testament, however, is widely rejected by men whose ability and scholarship cannot legitimately be called in question. The fact that so many scholars of high rank approve conclusions in the field of both Old and New Testament criticism, that necessitate the belief that the Bible contains numerous errors is, no doubt, an obstacle in the way of believing that it is completely trustworthy, but it falls far short of constituting irrefragable proof that such is the case.

4. Those who ascribe errors by the wholesale to the Bible do so on one or more of the grounds that have been mentioned. Those who speak of the Bible as trustworthy on the whole, or as in-

fallible in matters of faith and practice only, while they usually admit, or at least do not deny that the Bible contains scientific and historical errors, are accustomed in justification to point to such facts as the following. The writers of the Bible do not give precisely the same content or use precisely the same words in reporting an event or speech or expounding a doctrine and, in quoting Scripture, do not always quote it in precisely the same words and sense as the original. One tells us that the Bible is not inerrant because "no two evangelists agree in their report of the title on the cross, or in their account of the appearances of our Lord after the resurrection." Another argues that it is impossible to defend the inerrancy of the Bible because Exodus and Deuteronomy do not report the Ten Commandments in exactly the same words, because Matthew and Mark do not report the Beatitudes in the same words or even in the same sense, and because the four accounts of Peter's denial disagree not only verbally but as to the incidents that attended it. The ascription of errors to the Bible on such grounds, however, is due to a mistaken conception of what the Scriptures need to be in order to be fully trustworthy. It rests on the notion that to be fully trustworthy the Scriptures must be a sort of code, expressed in notarial form and with notarial exactness. As a matter of fact, all the representative defenders of the inerrancy of Scripture agree with Abraham Kuyper when he declares "that the writing down by the Holy Spirit of what was inspired has nothing in common with the protocolization of an authentic official report, but that the several events and truths, yea, the same events and truths in their many-sided significance, have been brought to the canvas by the Highest Artist with a diversity of color and many-sidedness of interpretation which may indeed confuse the near-sighted cabalist, but which by its delightful harmonies fills the master-student, standing at a distance, with heavenly raptures."[11] Such a mechanical, mathematical, code-like accuracy has never been ascribed to the Bible by any theologian worthy of the name and confessedly does not at all correspond to the actual character and contents of the Bible itself. There is no real warrant, therefore, for saying that the Bible contains errors because its contents are out of harmony with such a conception of Scripture. One could with equal warrant say that the Bible contains errors because it uses popular rather than scientific language—speaks for instance of the sun as rising and setting when every schoolboy knows that strictly speaking such is not the case.

5. Errors are often ascribed to the Bible when there is reasonable doubt as to whether the alleged errors were in the original manuscripts. No one claims that the copyists and translators have been kept from error. No doubt this consideration may be abused. It is abused when it is used as *asylum ignorantiae,* as an ever-ready refuge to which to flee when confronted with alleged Biblical errors.

[11] *Bibliotheca Sacra,* October 1904, p. 675.

We have no right to say that the alleged errors were absent from the original manuscripts in defiance of all sound textual criticism. Nevertheless it should be firmly maintained that this consideration is a legitimate one and that no one has a right to allege a Biblical error unless he can show beyond a reasonable doubt that it was in the original manuscript. This consideration is not a subterfuge, as is often said, but within proper limits an eminently reasonable one.

We would not be understood as asserting that, even after the fullest possible import has been allowed the five considerations mentioned above, there do not remain phenomena which with our present knowledge are not easy to reconcile with the Church doctrine of the Bible. It should be remembered, however, that the history of Biblical criticism warrants a presumption that advancing knowledge will vindicate the Bible. The "proved errors" that were most confidently paraded a generation or two ago by those who impugned the trustworthiness of the Bible are no longer mentioned. It is well to remember also that the Tubingen school of criticism, which a generation ago enjoyed about the same vogue as the Form Criticism school does today, has now only an historical interest. Such a fact warns us against supposing that the Bible necessarily contains errors because it does not square with the so-called "assured results" of a fashionable school of criticism. In the meantime, it is a truly amazing fact that notwithstanding the assaults that have been made on the Bible scholars of the first rank hold that there are no proved errors in the Bible.[12]

While it is conceivable that we *could* have a knowledge of Christianity without the Bible, there is little reason to think that we *would* have it, if it had not been given fixedness and durability through being committed to writing. According to the Church doctrine, the Bible contains both a record of the facts that lie at the basis of Christianity and an authoritative interpretation of them. The question of the degree to which the lowered views of the inspiration of the Bible permit of adherence to Christianity rightly so called hinges on the degree to which they permit of belief in those facts together with the Biblical interpretation of them. Some of the advocates of "naturalistic Christianity" have sought to distinguish between the facts of the Bible and the interpretation of them given by their authors, and have maintained that after the interpretation with its supernatural framework has been discarded there still remains

[12] The complete trustworthiness of the Bible is defended with unsurpassed scholarship by Warfield in *Inspiration and Authority of the Bible.* The volume consists of his collected writings—some of which are highly technical—on the inspiration of the Bible. More recent and more popular discussions are *The Inspiration of the Scriptures,* by Dr. L. Boettner and *Scripture Cannot Be Broken,* by Dr. Theodore Engelder. Among scholars of distinction who have not written books of the subject but who believe in the complete trustworthiness of the Bible may be mentioned. Dr. Oswald T. Allis, author of *The Five Books of Moses,* Dr. Ned B. Stonehouse, author of *The Witness of Matthew and Mark,* Dr. Wm. Childs Robinson, author of *Christ—The Hope of Glory,* and Dr. Cornelius Van Til, author of *The New Modernism.*

a residue of abiding value. Others of them have maintained that the facts and the interpretations are intertwined to such a degree that it is impossible to separate them, and so have rejected both. Advocates of Christianity rightly so called agree with those who maintain that it is impossible to separate the facts and doctrines but differ from them in that they accept both. Apart from its facts, Christianity, they hold, would be empty of content, as empty as astronomy would be if the stars were but phantoms. It is equally true, however, that apart from the doctrines there would be no such thing as what has been called Christianity for some 1900 years. If we give the facts no interpretation, they are meaningless. If we give them an interpretation other than that which the Bible gives them, they yield us something other than Christianity.

The writers upon whom we are dependent for the doctrines of Christianity are also the ones upon whom we are dependent for its facts. If we reject their interpretation of the facts as immediately from God, and so authoritative—as they claim—how shall we be able to trust their statements as to the occurrence of the facts themselves? If we cannot trust them when they affirm that their interpretation is not the result of mere human reflection on the facts, how can we trust them when they represent the facts themselves as supernatural? It would seem, then, that either we must trust them for both the facts and the interpretation of the facts or we must look upon Christianity as merely a product of the religious life of man.[13] What we are trying to bring out is that, since we are wholly dependent on Christ and the Apostles for our knowledge of the facts and doctrines of Christianity and since, as we have seen, Christ and His Apostles are the source of the Church doctrine of the Bible, we cannot reject the latter without undermining our confidence in their trustworthiness both as recorders of facts and as teachers of doctrine. This is why, logically at least, the lowered views of inspiration are fraught with such consequence. Our confidence in all the teachings of the Bible is affected. If we reject the testimony which the Bible offers to its own trustworthiness, what warrant is there for accepting its testimony on other matters? If a witness on the stand asserts that he was an eyewitness of an event which he relates, and it be proved that he was elsewhere when the event happened, will not his testimony on other matters be put in question? Is it supposable that the jury will judge that, though the witness lied when he said that he was an eyewitness of the event, that fact has no bearing on the value of his testimony on other matters? There is a sense, therefore, in which the case for Christianity is bound up with the case for the trustworthiness of the Scriptures. We are dependent upon the Scriptures for our knowledge of all the distinctive facts and doctrines of Christianity. If we cannot trust them when they tell us about themselves, how can we trust them when they tell us about the deity of Christ, redemption

[13] See pages 128-129.

in His blood, justification by faith, regeneration by the Holy Spirit, the resurrection of the body and life everlasting?

The gravity of the situation that is raised by the testimony of the Scriptures to their own nature is not adequately appreciated, however, unless it is perceived that the trustworthiness of Him to whom the Scriptures testify is involved. It is a firmly established exegetical fact that Jesus ascribed absolute authority to the Scriptures of the Old Testament and that He, humanly speaking, derived His conception of His life-task from those Scriptures. How then is it possible to escape the dilemma, now that the theory of accommodation is no longer reputable, either Jesus' view of the Old Testament is the correct one or Jesus Himself was mistaken? Thus the conflict over the Scriptures becomes a conflict over Christ Himself. It may be admitted that many who ascribe not only historical but moral faults to the Scriptures bow before Christ as Lord and rejoice in Him as their Saviour. But surely in the long run so inconsequential an attitude cannot be maintained. The logic of the situation is dead against those who are at the same time worshipers and critics of Christ. If we mistake not, it is ignorance or lack of thought that makes it possible for many to suppose that they can remain orthodox in their conception of Jesus while accepting many of the critical views that are widely current. As long as it remains true that the disciple is not above his master or the servant above his lord, so long will it remain true that men are at least imperfect disciples of Christ as long as they can say, "Jesus taught so and so, but the real truth of the matter is thus and thus." Here too we cannot escape the decisive question, What think ye of Christ?

"Prove all things; hold fast that which is good."—I THESS. 5:21.

CHAPTER IX

DEFORMATIONS AND FALSIFICATONS OF CHRISTIANITY

Among the extra-canonical sayings ascribed to Jesus, best entitled to be regarded as genuine, is the saying, "Show yourselves approved money-changers." Many of the Church fathers made use of this saying to explain Paul's injunction, "Prove all things: hold fast that which is good" (I Thess. 5:23), believing that underlying this exhortation is the figure of a money-changer testing the coins submitted to him to ascertain whether they are genuine or counterfeit. Whether or not this saying was an actual utterance of Jesus, and was present to Paul's mind when he penned his well-known injunction, it directs attention to a qualification much needed today by Christians and non-Christians alike.

Few things are more needed today than the ability to distinguish between genuine and counterfeit Christianity. In our opening chapter we directed attention to the number and diversity of the things called Christianity. All sorts of coins, bearing the image and superscription of Christianity, are in circulation. One of the results is that there are many persons calling themselves Christians—some who even pride themselves on the purity of their Christian confession—who are embracing systems of thought and life which lack all that is most essential to genuine Christianity. This book will have failed of its purpose if it does not prove effective, in some degree, in remedying this situation by helping the men of today distinguish between what is rightly and what is falsely called Christianity. In an age in which so many mutually opposed systems of thought and life fly the Christian flag, or at least assert that they are essentially Christian in character, there is no more pressing need than that to which Paul gave expression in his prayer for the Philippians (Phil. 1:9). As translated by Weymouth it reads: "It is my prayer that your love may be more and more accompanied by clear knowledge and keen perception for testing things that differ." Surely there is no difference of farther reaching importance than that between Christian and non-Christian thinking and living, and yet this distinction is blurred to such a degree today that many are at a loss to know what the thing rightly called Christianity really is.

In examining the coins in circulation bearing the image and superscription of Christianity, if we are to show ourselves approved money-changers, we must discriminate between those which, though defective, mutilated, or under-weight, are genuine and those which, whatever their appearance, are counterfeit. Such coins have, so to speak, been in circulation for nearly two thousand years. During that time many of them have become worn and defaced, some have been mutilated, some have had part of their gold removed and replaced with base metal, some have been melted down and reminted with more or less alloy added. This deformed currency, however, is not the same as counterfeit currency and should not be confused with it. Expressed in less figurative language, the deformations of Christianity—the result in large part of heresy and schism—are of an entirely different character from falsifications of Christianity.

The Deformations of Christianity

In dealing with the deformations of Christianity two extremes should be avoided—that of the indifferentists and that of the perfectionists or absolutists. The former ignore the difference between these deformations and so treat them as of equal value, while the latter are so fully convinced of the purity and integrity of their own type of Christianity that they anathematize all other types and reject them as worthless. No doubt it argues weakness of conviction to treat the differences between Protestant and Roman Catholic conceptions of Christianity as unimportant or even to treat the differences between Lutheran, Reformed and Wesleyan conceptions of Christianity—not to mention the differences between these and the Pietists and Pentecostals and others—as unimportant. On the other hand, it argues an excess of conviction to assume that the type of Christianity we accept is the only type that can be rightly so called and to treat all other types as falsifications.

It is not surprising, in view of the present-day attacks being made on Christianity both by open enemies and by false friends, that many sincere Christians think that the differences that separate the various evangelical denominations—even those that separate Protestants and Roman Catholics—are relatively trivial and that the need of the hour is that the various branches of the Christian faith forget their differences and join forces so that they may wage more effective war against the common enemy. But, fully as we believe that the divisions of Christianity are responsible for much of its weakness in the face of encroaching Modernism, we are far from supposing that the erasing of denominational differences and the formation of one great Church organization is our greatest or even our most immediate need. That is to overlook the intellectual nature of this conflict. If such an organization or such a union of forces were brought about at the cost of loyalty to Christian truth, it would create little more than a mob that would be utterly unable to defend itself against the intelligently conceived and scientifically applied attacks of modern naturalism—whether in its more materialistic or its more pantheistic forms. Let us by all means seek a closer union of the forces of Christianity but let us not suppose that we can get along without a world and life view of our own. We must place principle over against principle, world view over against world view, if we are to prevail in what has rightly been called the greatest war of intellect since the birthday of the Nazarene. Eclectic, halfway, split-the-difference systems will not suffice. As Abraham Kuyper said more than a quarter of a century ago in words that have gained rather than lost significance with the passing years: "As truly as every plant has a root, so truly does a principle hide under every manifestation of life. These principles are interconnected and have their root in a fundamental principle; and from the latter is developed, logically and systematically, the whole complex of ruling ideas that go to make up our life and world view. With such a coherent world and life view, firmly resting on its principle and self-consistent in its splendid structure, Modernism now confronts Christianity; and against this deadly foe, ye Christians cannot successfully defend your sanctuary but by placing, in opposition to all this, a life and world view of your own, founded firmly on the base of your own principle, wrought out with the same clearness, and glittering in an equally logical consistency." [1]

While unqualified commendation cannot be given to those who so stress the consensus among Christians as to practically ignore their dissension, it is equally true that unqualified commendation cannot be given to those who are so enamored with their own interpretation of Christianity that they condemn all interpretations not closely related to it as fatally heretical. This means that the distinction between deformations and falsifications of Christianity is important. Our main concern is with the falsifications rather than the deformations of Christianity. We are far from being unconcerned, however, about the deformations. Christian Irenics is the study of the doc-

[1] *Lectures on Calvinism* (Wm. B. Eerdmans Pub. Co.), p. 284.

trinal differences of Christians for the purpose of harmonizing them. It stresses the consensus of opinion and tends to minimize the differences. Christian Polemics, on the other hand, is a study of the differences with the end in view of maintaining the articles of faith of one group over against all others. It stresses the difference of opinion and tends to ignore the consensus. There is a place and an important place for both in Christian thinking. The truly Christian position, we are convinced, is somewhere between those who know little or nothing but Irenics and those who know little or nothing but Polemics. The two should ever be found together. It is hard to say which extreme is the worst.

In the age in which we live Christian Irenics is in better repute than Christian Polemics but there have been other ages—for instance, that of the sixteenth and seventeenth centuries in which the opposite has been the case. Both extremes have been and are unfruitful of good and productive of evil. The tendency to stress the consensus and to soft-pedal the differences indicates ignorance of or unconcern over the fact that, whatever else Christianity is, it is a revelation of the truth. Those who lack the courage to defend what they regard as Christian truth can hardly be classed with the Christian heroes. What is more, if we confess only what those calling themselves Christians confess in common, our creed will necessarily be a brief one. At the best it will not contain the maximum of Christian content. At the worst it will retain nothing distinctive of Christianity at all, seeing that there is hardly a fact or doctrine of Christianity which is not denied or at least questioned by those in repute as Christians. But even if our creed retains something more than the minimum of Christianity it will not be a creed that can hope to contend with any hope of success against those today who reject the creed *in toto*. We are disposed to think that at present Christianity is suffering far more from Irenics than from Polemics but, if so, that is only because it is more widespread. There is great need, we believe, of a revival of Polemics, not however of a Polemics that has no appreciation of the truth contained in deformations of Christianity other than its own. We express ourselves advisedly when we say "deformations other than its own" because few things are more certain than that every confession of Christianity including our own is in some degree a deformed Christianity.

The best interest of Christianity will not be served, it seems to us, by the various circles of Christian thought ignoring their differences. These differences are important and to think otherwise is to put ourselves among those who having eyes see not and having ears hear not. It will be best served, we are convinced, if each, with due appreciation of the elements of Christian truth confessed by others, seeks to commend what is distinctive of itself. It is a serious error to suppose that all controversy is folly. Christ and His Apostles opposed error. It is hardly fitting therefore for His later disciples to condemn it wholly. What is more, in the great crises of Christianity such as occurred in the second, fifth and sixteenth centuries it has ever been sturdy contenders for the faith not theological pacifists who have saved the day. Everything depends upon the spirit in which the controversy is carried on. No doubt, controversy for its own sake or controversy carried on in a fault-finding spirit with a lack of fairness to opponents is harmful. But controversy need not be of that sort. Carried on with a sincere desire to further the truth rather than from the desire to refute an opponent, the clash of opinion that results will ever tend to promote a better understanding of Christianity on the part of all concerned.

Our main concern, however, as stated above, is with the falsifications of Christianity—the contrast between Christianity rightly so called and Christianity falsely so called. If we have said relatively little about the deformations that does not mean that we regard them as unimportant. But whatever the differences between the various deformations—we have previously expressed the view that all present-day expressions of Christianity are in some degree deformed—they are small compared with the difference between all that can rightly be called Christianity and everything that can not.

The most marked difference between these deformations is that between the Evangelicalism of Protestantism and the Sacerdotalism of Greek and Roman Catholicism. But great as is the difference between Evangelicalism and Sacerdotalism—

a difference that has to do with the question whether God in saving men deals with them directly or only through the medium of the means of grace He has established and committed to the Church for administration—it is by no means as great as that which separates both from a Liberalism or Modernism that knows nothing of the supernatural activity of God in the saving of the soul. While Evangelicals and Sacerdotalists differ in their conception of the way in which the power of God operates in saving the soul, both are supernaturalists in their conception of the plan of salvation inasmuch as they both hold that ultimately all the power employed in saving the soul is from God. It should not be overlooked, in this connection, that Protestantism, according to its own claims, originated in the *reformation* of an old, not in the formation of a new Christianity. Consequently there is a basic similarity between the historic Protestant and the Roman Catholic world and life view. Protestantism greatly modified the Roman Catholic view but it retained its general structure. As Herman Bavinck put it: "In their view of the world and life, sin and grace, heaven and hell, Church and State, faith and knowledge, Luther, Zwingli and Calvin were children of the Middle Ages and revealed this fact at every point of their activity as Reformers." [2] If Lutheran and Reformed Protestants have so much in common with Roman Catholics as over against a naturalistic Liberalism or Modernism that denies the supernatural foundation on which both build, it goes

[2] *The Philosophy of Revelation*, p. 4.

without saying that they have much more in common with those sharing their Evangelicalism who belong to Churches and sects that have originated since the Reformation.

The Falsifications of Christianity

We have touched upon the need and value of Polemics—of controversy if you will—having to do with the differences within what is rightly called Christianity. We have done this because we believe that a Christianity indifferent to these differences will be so weak and flabby that it will have neither the zeal nor the ability to hold in check, still less to turn back, those who improperly fly the flag of Christianity, not to mention those who repudiate Christianity in name as well as in fact. Our chief concern, however, is with the differences between what is rightly called Christianity and what is falsely called Christianity. It is the wide and bottomless chasm that yawns between these and not the gorges and gullies and such like that divide and sub-divide the more or less imperfect expressions of Christianity with which we are immediately concerned. This can be done rather briefly because it merely involves the use of those features of Christianity to which we have been directing attention as touchstones by which to distinguish between Christianity rightly so called and Christianity falsely so called. Some of the things called Christianity lack all the features we have emphasized but nothing, we believe, that lacks any of them has any right to call itself Christianity. This will be disputed by many. They will allege that they have as good right to use the name as we have. To make good this claim they will have to present adequate historical justification. That, we are sure, they cannot do. Hence, we believe, we are fully warranted in employing these features as tests to ascertain whether the things being called Christianity are really such. Ability to undergo these tests will not prove that they are one hundred per cent Christian—additional tests may be needed to ascertain their purity and adequacy—but inability to do so will make clear that they are something other than Christianity rightly so called.

Christianity rightly so called, as we have seen, involves the reality of the supernatural in the form of a personal God Who exists outside and beyond and above nature. Few of those calling themselves Christians deny the existence of the supernatural in this sense. Hence this fact is of relatively little value in distinguishing between Christianity rightly so called and Christianity falsely so called. And yet there are not lacking those calling themselves Christians who do not have such a reality in mind when they speak of the supernatural. Some regard men as supernatural beings. As understood by them, the supernatural is synonymous with the personal, and the distinction between the supernatural and the natural is merely the distinction between moral freedom and physical necessity—in other words between spirit and matter. When such speak of the supernatural they mean at the most the superhuman, and need not mean even that. Others—Christian Scientists, for instance—think of God abstractly as "Mind, Soul, Spirit, Principle" rather than concretely as a person, and, in harmony with this, they maintain, after the manner of the Pantheists, the essential oneness of God and men. Nothing is more certain, however, than that Christianity recognizes a radical distinction between the supernatural and the natural, and hence that any and every thing that erases this distinction between the supernatural God and the world He has created, whether material or spiritual, is something other than Christianity rightly so called. This does not mean, it should be needless to say, that Christianity sets no store by the natural. The Christian notion of the supernatural assumes the reality of the natural, seeing that there could be no *super*natural if there were no natural. It is not to be supposed that Christianity is an anti-natural religion. It no more maintains that everything is supernatural than it maintains that everything is natural. It is rather natural religion to which has been added what is needed to make it a religion suited to the needs of men in the unnatural condition brought about by sin. It does not deny or minimize the reality or efficiency of second causes. It stands mid-way between pure naturalism and pure supernaturalism.[3]

We have also seen that Christianity rightly so called involves the reality of the supernatural in the form of the miraculous. It is particularly important to keep this in mind because of the large

[3] See pages 131-132.

number of those calling themselves Christians for whom the supernatural in this form does not exist. Relatively few of them, as we have said, deny the existence of a supernatural God but the number of those who deny that this supernatural God has intervened miraculously in the affairs of this world are legion. These miracles include miracles in both the narrow and the broad sense of the word. Miracles, in the narrow sense of the word, include those mighty acts that God has wrought in the external world for this world's redemption—acts which culminate in the events connected with the Person and work of Jesus Christ. In the broad sense of the word, miracles also include the acts and works of God in the spiritual world such as regeneration and sanctification by means of which sinners are restored to newness of life and the tendencies to evil within them are progressively eradicated and holy dispositions implanted, nourished and perfected.

Somewhere mid-way between miracles in the narrow and broad sense of the word stands the death of Jesus Christ as a sacrifice for sin. It was an event in the external world and yet it was much more an event in the spiritual world. However we may class it among the wonderful works of God, it contributes so largely to the making of Christianity what it is that, apart from it, Christianity as it is set forth in the New Testament and as it finds expression in all the great creeds of the Churches, would not exist. It cannot be said too emphatically that genuine Christianity does not exist where it is not recognized that Christianity is a redemptive religion that offers salvation from the guilt and corruption of sin through the atoning death of Jesus Christ. The object of the Christian's faith has ever been not merely Jesus Christ conceived as the God-man, it has always been Jesus Christ as crucified. An atoning death of Christ is just as indispensable to Christianity as a divine Christ. A Christless Christianity is no more a contradiction in words than a non-atoning Christ is a contradiction in fact. Christianity involves the acknowledgment of Christ not only as Lord and God but specifically as that One Who bore our sins in His own body on the tree.

Test Questions

We submit that none have any right to call what they confess Christianity unless they can answer affirmatively the following questions: Do you believe in a supernatural God Who is Creator and Ruler of all things visible and invisible? Do you believe in a Christianity that is based upon and constituted by certain great historical facts, more particularly upon the fact of Christ as One to Whom it owes both its origin and its continuance? Does the fact of the death of Christ as an atoning sacrifice occupy a central place among these constitutive facts? Does what you call Christianity posit the absolute need of regeneration and sanctification by the Holy Spirit, the Third Person of the Trinity? Inability to answer these questions in the affirmative will make clear that what they call Christianity is a falsification of it. We would not be understood as implying that the ability to answer them affirmatively proves that the Christianity confessed is adequate Christianity. It may still be a deformation of Christianity, either by reason of additions or subtractions, but we may be sure that it is a phase of Christianity.

In applying these tests to the things called Christianity today we wish to avoid, as far as possible, applying them in such a way as to pass judgment on individuals. Neither breadth and accuracy of knowledge nor logical capacity nor consistency of thought are conditions of salvation. Men are often better than their creeds so that deep in the core of their being there may be a better faith than they have expressed in words. It does not seem to us, however, that the injunction "judge not that ye not be judged" applies to views and opinions that have been formulated in words. Let us, then, proceed to indicate what the application of these tests reveals concerning some, at least, of the things being taught by those calling themselves Christians.

In the first place, the application of these tests makes clear that Liberalism and Modernism—whether regarded as different names for the same thing or as having somewhat different connotations—in as far as they commend a purely naturalistic conception of Christianity are falsifications of Christianity. Fortunately all those ordinarily spoken of as Liberals or Modernists do not commend a purely naturalistic conception of Christianity, but Liberalism and Modernism in all their consistent forms of expression commend types of religious belief that are not only basically diverse from Christianity rightly so called but that are particularly deceptive by reason of their use of traditional Christian terminology. That any and all purely naturalistic conceptions of Christianity are something other than Christianity rightly so called is so obvious that it seems strange that anybody ever supposed otherwise. It goes without saying that such a Christianity is a non-miraculous Christianity and hence that the only Bible it can accept is an exclusively human Bible and the only Christ in which it can believe is a Christ who can be enclosed in human moulds. The most that its adherents can believe concerning Jesus is that he was the founder of what they call Christianity, the one who set it going, its classic teacher and example from whom they draw inspiration and encouragement in their own religious living. At the most, Jesus is for such the first Christian, the first in that long line of persons who have believed as he believed and endeavored to live as he lived. They may say with Rudolf Eucken, "we can revere him as a leader, a hero, a martyr," but the logic of the situation inevitably demands that they add as does Eucken, "but we cannot forthwith bind and pledge ourselves to him and yield him unconditional submission; still less can we make him the center of a cult, for that would be nothing less than intolerable idolatry."[4] Small wonder that in the concluding paragraph of his

[4] *Can We Still Be Christians?* (The Macmillan Co.), p. 34.

book *Can We Still Be Christians?* Eucken wrote: "Our question was whether we can still be Christians. Our answer is that we not only can but must be Christians—only, however, on the one condition that Christianity be recognized as a progressive historic movement still in the making, that it be shaken free from the numbing influence of ecclesiasticism and placed upon a broader foundation"—that is to say, on condition that it be a radically different Christianity from that which has hitherto borne the name. Sad to say, there are many today who follow Eucken's example. They say, in effect, that they cannot believe in a Christianity that places the once crucified but now glorified Son of God at its center but that they will call what they can believe Christianity and be satisfied with that. Such reasoning, we are frank to say, seems to us not only unsound but dishonest. We much prefer the blunt assertion of D. F. Strauss, one of the ablest of the forerunners of current Modernism who at the close of his life put the question, "Are we still Christians?" and answered with an explicit "No." Surely those whose interest is in realities rather than mere names will agree.

It has become so common today, even in genuinely Christian circles, to speak of Jesus as a Christian that it may be well to reassert how thoroughly *unchristian* such a mode of speech is. If Jesus was a Christian He was merely the first of that series of believers we call Christians. In that case He is no more a proper object of worship than Peter and John and Paul or even than Augustine and Aquinas and Luther and Wesley. Such a mode of speech erases the difference between the servant and his Lord, between the sinner and his Saviour. It implies that Jesus Himself does not belong to the essential content of Christianity any more than Luther belongs to the essential content of Lutheranism or Wesley to the essential content of Methodism. A Christianity, however, that could even conceivably get along without Jesus is something other than Christianity rightly so called. Jesus was not a Christian; He was and is the Christ, the Saviour of the world, the Lord and Life of humanity.

In the second place, these tests make clear that all interpretations of Christianity consistent with Rationalism and Mysticism (spelled with capital letters) lack what is distinctive of Christianity rightly so called. Neither Rationalism nor Mysticism attaches any abiding and indispensable significance to historic facts, events that happened in time and space. They may and do hold that such facts or events have symbolic or illustrative value, but constitutive significance they do not ascribe to them. Whatever be the difference between Rationalism and Mysticism—the difference is not so great as is often supposed, being much a matter of temperament as indicated by the saying "the rationalist blows cold, the mystic hot; warm up a rationalist and you get a mystic; cool down a mystic and you get a rationalist"—they are wholly at one in affirming that religion is basically independent of historic facts.

Rationalists endlessly repeat the saying of Lessing that "accidental truths of history can never be the proof of necessary truths of reason." It is "eternal truths," those that have always been true and not those that became true in time as actual history, that alone are essential according to the Rationalist. The Rationalists may admit that Christianity is entangled with history, they may even admit that apart from this entanglement it would not have been able to survive its infancy, but they unhesitatingly assert that these historical elements are not permanently essential to it. Mystics follow a somewhat different route but arrive at essentially the same destination. They too will have nothing vital to do with history. They too claim the ability to derive from their own inalienable endowments the whole of what is essential to religion. They too may not deny the reality of the facts upon which historic Christianity bases itself but they sublimate them into symbols of inward experiences. For example, the Mystic does not say that the salvation of mankind depends on what happened on Calvary but rather that what happened on Calvary was the supreme manifestation of that spirit of sacrifice on which the salvation of mankind depends. According to the Mystic Jesus Himself was a Mystic of exceptional purity and energy, and Paul and the other Apostles somewhat lesser but none the less outstanding Mystics. Evelyn Underhill writes: "The examination of Christian origins from the psychological point of view suggests that Christianity began as a Mystical movement of the purest kind; that its Founder and those who succeeded Him possessed the characteristically Mystical consciousness and passed through the normal stages of Mystical growth."[5]

In affirming that all interpretations of Christianity consistent with Rationalism and Mysticism, spelled with capital letters, are false, we do not mean to imply for a moment that Christianity is not a reasonable religion or that it is not in any sense a mystical religion. While Christianity rejects the primary assumption of Rationalism, *viz.*, the ability of human reason to produce out of itself the whole body of religious truth which it is necessary or desirable for mankind to embrace, yet it claims to be a rational not an irrational religion, and does not hesitate to maintain that any and all religions should be denied a hearing in the court of feeling once they have been non-suited at the bar of reason. But if Christianity claims to be a rational though not a rationalistic religion it is equally true it is a mystical religion without being Mysticism (spelled with a capital letter). It is of the very essence of Christianity that God has immediate access to the human soul and that the Christian enjoys direct communion with God—a communion that includes communion with the living Christ. If the Christian is shocked by those who profess to know God apart from Christ, he is equally shocked by those

[5] *The Mystic Way*, Preface, p. 8.

who deny the possibility of communion with the exalted Christ.

In the third place, these tests make clear that nothing is rightly called Christianity which teaches that men are saved on the basis of what they are or what they have done. If Christianity be, as we have maintained, a redemptive religion in the sense that it offers salvation from the guilt and corruption of sin through the atoning death of Jesus Christ and the regenerating and sanctifying influence of the Holy Spirit, it is to deny what lies at its very heart to allege that man can save himself.[6] It has been the constant testimony of the universal Church that salvation is from God and from God alone, however much a different conception may, from time to time, have prevailed among its members. This does not mean that Christianity is indifferent to what a man is or to what he does. Rather it is its concern for these things that explains its insistence that salvation is from God, not from man. It holds that man because of his sin is utterly unable to accomplish his own salvation, that he must be quickened into newness of life before he can become what he ought to be or do what he ought to do. It admits that the unrenewed sinner may suppress sin at this point and that but it will inevitably break out at some other point. Moralism, whether of the Sadducean or Pharisaic, whether of the Greek or Hebrew type, has never saved a single human soul. It is not necessary for our purpose to prove that

[6] See pages 63 ff.

this is true. All we need to do is to point out that this is what Christianity teaches. We may or may not approve its teachings. Be that as it may, nothing that is rightly called Christianity teaches salvation by character or upon the basis of good works. Christianity looks forward to the day when men shall be morally perfect but in the meantime Christians ever say to one another in the words of Paul: "By grace are ye saved through faith; and that not of yourselves: it is the gift of God: not of works lest any man should boast." However, they do not fail to add with Paul "for we are His workmanship, created in Christ Jesus unto good works" (Eph. 2:8-10).

Such are some of the results we obtain when we put the test questions we have enumerated to the things called Christianity. Other applications of them may be made by the reader. It is obvious, for instance, that Unitarianism, Christian Science, Unity and Russellism as commended by the Jehovah Witnesses are not Christianity rightly so called inasmuch as their advocates cannot and do not answer these questions in the affirmative. These tests may and should be applied to the teaching of individuals, both within and without the organized Churches. It is not enough that they answer some of these questions in the affirmative. They must be able to answer them all in the affirmative in order to justify any claim they may make to be exponents of what can rightly be called Christianity. In applying these tests to individuals, in distinction from their teachings, it should ever be kept in mind, as has already been pointed out, that neither fullness of knowledge nor logical capacity is a condition of salvation. To deny Unitarianism, Christian Science, not to mention other organizations, the right to call themselves Christian organizations is not necessarily to deny that there are Christians within these organizations.

It may have been noticed that we have not made use of the ethical test despite the fact that we have represented the ethics of Christianity as one of its outstanding marks or characteristics.[7] It seems to us, however, that this test is so difficult of application as to be of little use in distinguishing between what is really Christianity and what is merely called Christianity. Its use here is greatly limited by the fact that practically all of those calling themselves Christians profess to accept the ethics of Christianity. What is more, the fact that even the best of Christians exemplify the ethics of Christianity so inadequately, and the average Christian so poorly, makes it practically impossible, on the basis of conduct alone, to decide whether what he professes is Christianity rightly so called. It should be remembered also that even those who make no profession of Christianity have, in our own country at least, been reared in a society that is more or less pervaded by Christian ideals of conduct so that, superficially considered, there is often little difference between the conduct of Christians and non-Christians. The situation is

7 See pages 51 and 84 ff.

further complicated by the fact that there are those whose lives do not correspond to their Christian profession. The question these raise, however, is not, Is the Christianity they profess rightly so called? but rather, Are they really Christians? In view of such considerations, the ethical test can be used negatively better than it can be used positively. We may be sure that any and everything that is hostile to or indifferent to the Christian ethic is something other than Christianity, but that is about as far as we can safely go.

If Christianity has, as we have maintained, a definite content—a content that was given it once and for all by Christ and His Apostles—it should be clear to all that much of what is called Christianity today is not rightly so called. Men are everywhere giving up the substance but not the name of Christianity. Why? Apparently the explanation is found in the fact that Christianity is still a name to conjure with. This is much to the credit of Christianity but highly discreditable to those who employ the name to designate what is quite different from what for some 1900 years has borne the name. It is clearly a case of sailing under a false flag, of infringing on a competitor's trademark, of squatting on another man's property. We do not question the right, however we may question the wisdom, of holding and advocating what lacks the distinctive marks of historic Christianity. We do, however, question the right to call it Christianity. Honest terminology forbids it.

"I am the way, the truth, and the life: no man cometh unto the Father but by me."—JOHN 14:6.

CHAPTER X

THE TRUTH AND FINALITY OF CHRISTIANITY

Our primary purpose in this book is expository—to show what is and what is not Christianity rightly so called. Any defensive or apologetic elements that may have crept in have been purely incidental to our main purpose. In taking up the matter of the truth and finality of Christianity, our purpose is the same—not to defend its truthfulness and finality but rather to indicate what is meant when we speak of the truth of Christianity and to point out that the finality of Christianity is bound up with the question of its truthfulness.

When we speak of the truth of Christianity we have in mind, of course, Christianity as we have defined it. It is no comfort to us to have a man tell us that he believes that Christianity is true if, on interrogating him, we find that what he calls Christianity lacks all that is most distinctive of what we call Christianity. Because in that case, if what he calls Christianity is true, what we call Christianity is false. Christianity, according to many calling themselves Christians, is a religion in which Jesus is merely an example of saving faith, not its object, and His death merely the death of a martyr, not of a sacrificial victim. If what these call Christianity were true, it would not only mean that what we call Christianity is basically false but would impinge upon our belief that Christianity is the only true religion. It is the truth of that particular redemptive religion that offers salvation from the guilt and corruption of sin through the atoning death of Jesus Christ and the regenerating and sanctifying activity of the Holy Spirit that we have in mind when we speak of the truth of Christianity, not the truth of every religion that may label itself Christianity. It is necessary to insist on this in view of the looseness with which the word, Christianity, is frequently employed today. Obviously it evacuates the word of all definite meaning to employ it to designate things diametrically opposed to each other—as is done when it is used to designate the views of those who do and those who not see in Jesus Christ an object of worship or of those who do and those who do not ground their hope in the conviction that He bore their sins in His own body on the tree. It is regrettable that the word as currently employed so often lacks definite meaning but what is far more regrettable is the absence from the thoughts and lives of so many calling themselves Christians of the thing for which the word unquestionably stood until comparatively recent times. The loss of the word as an unambiguous designation of the religion we profess would be a matter of small concern if the thing which the word once unambiguously expressed was not only being retained but expanding in its influence. The retention of the word itself affords us satisfaction only as the thing it once everywhere denoted is retained, as those who are interested in realities more than words will understand.

When we speak of the truth of Christianity we mean, in the next place, that it is true in both the sense of "truth of fact" and "truth of idea." In asserting that Christianity is true in the sense of "truth of fact" we mean to affirm that it is a religion that is based upon facts that actually happened and so to deny that it is a religion whose value is independent of history. In asserting that Christianity is true in the sense of "truth of idea," we mean to affirm that its doctrines, principles and ideals are eternally valid. Strange as it may seem to ordinary, common-sense people, there are many alleged Christian leaders who maintain that Christianity is true only in the sense of truth of idea. Facts, they would have us believe, have significance only as they express or illustrate some idea or principle. The idea or principle, they tell us, is the principal thing and, provided we grasp that, it is a matter of little or no moment whether the "fact" that expresses or illustrates it is real or fictitious. Somewhat as the value of the Parable of the Prodigal Son is the same whether the father and son of the parable be regarded as real or fictitious or as the parable of the Good Samaritan is the same whether or not the events it records actually happened, so, we are told, the value of the Bible is essentially the same whether Abraham and Jacob and Moses and Jesus be actual historical characters, having the reality that attaches to historical figures like Caesar and Alexander and Lincoln, or whether they are merely ideal characters having only the reality of a character in a modern drama or novel. Edification, judgment of value, moral and spiritual instruction, not objective history or science, such tell us, is the main concern of the Bible. In harmony with this they tell us that the value of Christianity, the religion that finds expression in its pages, is independent of the question whether the facts upon which it has long been supposed to be based are true in the sense in which the scientist and the historian understand truth. We have previously dealt at some length with this matter. There is no need to repeat here what was said there.[1] Suffice it to say that, as we view it, unless the facts of Christianity be real facts, Christianity is as empty of content as the science of astronomy would be if the stars were phantoms and that unless the interpretation of those facts given us in the Bible be the true interpretation, our conception of what Christianity is, is so vague and indefinite, if not positively erroneous, as to make it doubtful whether it is worthy of our serious consideration. As we view it, we must have both the facts and the doctrines if we are to have on our hands Christianity as it appears in the New Testament and as it finds expression in all the great historic creeds. Hence when we speak of the truth of Christianity we have in mind its truth both in the sense of "truth of fact" and "truth of idea."

[1] See pages 114 ff.

Again when we speak of the truth of Christianity we mean that it is absolutely, not merely relatively, true. Many maintain that because Christianity is an historical religion it is necessarily historically conditioned in such a way that it can be only relatively true. Such a notion, however, rests, we believe, upon an anti-theistic or at least inadequately theistic view of the universe. It assumes that the universe, including man, exists more or less independently of God and that when He desired to make a word-revelation to mankind He was compelled to pick out the best instrument He could find among the children of men.[2] Since even the best instrument discoverable was imperfect this would mean that the revelation itself would be necessarily imperfect. According to an adequate theism, however, nothing exists independently of God, the Creator and Ruler of all things visible and invisible. God could, therefore, prepare just the instrument that was needed for the purpose in hand. Hence the product could partake of the perfection of God Himself. If Christianity is based upon certain supernatural facts plus their true interpretation, as we have contended, it is absolutely not merely relatively true. Facts do not lose their significance with passage of time. Reality once made is made forever. The circumstance that the facts upon which Christianity is based happened nearly two thousand years ago does not affect their value today. The only question that need concern us today is whether the

2 See pages 199 ff.

facts alleged to have happened in the long ago have the significance that the New Testament attached to them. If the interpretation there given is but the product of mere human reflection upon them it is not necessarily definitive. It is quite possible in that case that the interpretation there given is capable of improvement or even that it should be set aside in favor of another and different interpretation. But if it be, as the New Testament writers themselves alleged, that God Himself is the Author of the interpretation there given and that the meaning there given is their meaning for God Himself, that interpretation is the true interpretation in the absolute sense of the word. If the facts alleged to have happened actually happened and if the interpretation of their meaning which we have is their meaning for God—as the vast majority of those calling themselves Christians have believed and still do believe—then Christianity is true not merely relatively but absolutely. At least, this is what we mean to affirm when we speak of the truth of Christianity.

Obviously when we speak of the truth of Christianity we do not merely mean that it is useful. We believe indeed that it has proved its usefulness in bringing not only peace and comfort and inspiration to individuals but in changing social and economic and political conditions. Its Founder expected it to prove its usefulness as is indicated by the fact that He gave His approval to the principle embodied in the words, "By their fruits ye shall know them." It may even be said that if

Christianity had not shown itself to be useful it would long ago have ceased to have any interest, unless perhaps for antiquarians. It has been useful, however, only because it has been believed to be true. While there is force in the pragmatic argument, "Christianity is useful and therefore true," yet, if it should be proven to be false, we may be sure that this argument would at once lose its force. Basically, its usefulness, pragmatists to the contrary notwithstanding, depends upon its truthfulness. It could hardly be otherwise in view of the fact that the manner of life which it inculcates whether for the individual or society is based upon a message—a message which involves a world view in which such things as sin regarded as guilt and corruption, redemption in and through the once crucified but now living Lord and Saviour, the supernatural activity of the Holy Spirit in regenerating and sanctifying sinners, heaven and hell, occupy an essential and determining place. That being the case, the question of the truthfulness of Christianity is the question of primary importance. Whatever benefits may flow from Christianity, it is "useful" in the full sense in which it claims to be useful only as the Christian message has to do with actual not supposed realities. Judgments of value are dependent upon judgments of fact. What is more, Christianity refuses to be regarded as a mere means to some higher end. To accept Christianity merely as a means of securing a better and more law abiding community or a unified nation or international peace or such like is to reject it. Jesus said, "Seek ye first the kingdom of God and His righteousness, and all these things shall be added unto you," but if we seek the kingdom of God and His righteousness merely in order to get "these things," that is to say, material blessings, we will miss both them and the Kingdom of God.

Is Christianity true in the sense indicated? It is foreign to our purpose to endeavor to prove that it is. It may not be out of place, however, for us to mention the fact that it has always been so contended by the Christian Church. In that conviction it was established, in that conviction it has grown, and only as that conviction is maintained, we make bold to say, can it escape decay and go on from strength to strength. However much men may try to conceal it, the fundamental reason for the present-day defection from Christianity, especially in academic circles, is that men have been led to believe that Christianity is not true. If Christianity is to shape the future, it will do so because men continue to maintain, as all the great heroes of the Christian faith have maintained, that the Christian is the only true rationalist. Christians are not irrationalists. Such a charge has no basis in fact. Reason, while it has not escaped the influence of sin, has its necessary place in grasping and understanding truth. As a result, Christianity will not long continue to move the hearts and guide the hands of men after it is no longer approved by their heads. This being the case, the task of convincing many of the present age that they have been overhasty in concluding that Christianity is not true in the sense indicated may not be shirked. It is true that rational assent does not of itself make a man a Christian. To be a Christian is much more than to have an intellectual conviction of the truthfulness of Christianity. "The devils also believe—and tremble." It is futile, however, to expect a rational being to become a Christian as long as he withholds rational assent. "Believe on the Lord Jesus Christ and thou shalt be saved,"we are told, but such advice is worthy of the consideration of intelligent beings only if there is adequate warrant for believing that Jesus Christ exists as a living reality, both able and willing to save those who put their trust in Him. Christians are not such merely because they find it comforting to believe in the existence of a Father-God and a Saviour-King. Not at all. They are such because it is the only reasonable as well as the only wise thing to be. Otherwise Christian piety and devotion are children of ignorance and Christian churches asylums for the feeble-minded. Because we cannot argue a man into becoming a Christian it does not follow that there is no need of presenting arguments at all. How frequently the words are cited: "He argued not, but preached, and conscience did the rest." No doubt a clear statement of what Christianity is is often the best argument in its favor; but it is also true that often something more is needed. While only the Holy Spirit can make a man a real Christian—"Verily, verily I say unto you," said the Christ, "ye must be born again"—yet it is not a blind ungrounded faith that the Holy Spirit works in the sinner. Paul may plant and Apollos water; it is God alone Who gives the increase. That is not to say, however, that it is a matter of no moment whether Paul plants and Apollos waters. In all ages there have been those set for the defense as well as for the proclamation of the gospel; and who will say that their work has not been greatly used of God? Surely, if there were need of Christian apologists in the past, there is need of them today in view of the fact that we have no knowledge of an age or generation in Europe and America in which Christianity rightly so called was more widely repudiated and even spoken against than the one in which we live.

A word in conclusion as to the question of the finality of Christianity. Does Christianity represent but one stage—even though it be the highest yet reached—in the religious development of mankind? Or does it represent the final stage in that development, so that no matter what the future may have in store for the religious history of mankind, Christianity will be found to be not only unsurpassed but unsurpassable? In other words, Is Christianity destined like the religions of Egypt and Assyria and Greece and Rome, not to mention others, to take up its abode with the dead or is it continuously to renew its strength and thus abide essentially the same until the end of time?

The answer to be given to the questions just put, and questions such as these, depends upon the answer we give to the prior question, Is Christianity true? This appears the moment we consider its claims. There can be no doubt but that Christianity claims finality. This being the case, the question of its finality is inextricably bound up with the question of its truthfulness. This claim to finality was made explicitly both by its Founder and those Whom He appointed to be its first teachers and preachers. Witness the words of Jesus: "All things have been delivered unto me of my Father: and no one knoweth the Son save the Father; neither doth any one know the Father save the Son, and he to whomsoever the Son willeth to reveal Him" (Matt. 11:27), "I am the way, and the truth and the life; no one cometh unto the Father but by me" (John 14:6). Witness also the words of Peter: "And in none other is there salvation; for neither is there any other name under heaven, that is given among men, wherein ye must be saved" (Acts 4:12); also those of Paul: "Other foundation can no man lay than that which is laid, which is Jesus Christ" (I Cor. 3:11) and "There is one God, one mediator also between God and men, himself man, Christ Jesus" (I Tim. 2:5). Even if such explicit statements were lacking, it would be clear that the question of the finality of Christianity is but an extension of the question of its truthfulness. It is involved in its character as a redemptive religion, particularly in the fact that it commends Jesus not as the first and best example of saving faith but as its object. If Jesus were but the first and best example of saving faith He would not be the only Saviour. In that case there might be many saviours—at the most He would only be the most effective. If, however, it be true, as Christianity alleges, that by reason of sin men lack the power to save themselves, a mere teacher and example cannot meet their deepest need. Under such conditions what men primarily need is not a teacher and example but a veritable Saviour, One to Whom they can look for that which they lack and yet without which they are undone. If now Jesus Christ is not only such a Saviour but the only such Saviour conceivable, as Christianity claims, it must be that Christianity is the final religion provided there is any possibility of salvation.

It is highly important to note that it is a supernatural not a natural redemption that Christianity professes to offer. Such a redemptive religion having God as its Author, provided it is true, is necessarily the final religion. As a supernatural redemptive religion, finality belongs to the very essence of Christianity. Hence any abatement of Christianity's claim to finality involves a denial of its truthfulness. Its claim to finality stands or falls with its supernaturalism. Only a supernatural religion could be a final religion. Naturalists, needless to say, do not believe in the finality of Christianity. The same is true, however, of "supernaturalists" of the pantheistic type, *i.e.*, those who obliterate the sharp distinction between the natural and the supernatural by alleging that all revelation is supernatural from the viewpoint of its source in God but natural from the viewpoint of its mode of occurrence. A man may even be a supernaturalist of the theistic type without believing in the finality of Christianity unless he holds that Christianity is a product of the supernatural in the form of the miraculous. It is even possible for one to believe in a religion that is the product of the supernatural in the form of the miraculous without believing that such a religion possesses finality. Judaism was such a religion. However Judaism did not claim finality. It looked forward to a fulfillment in the future. Christianity, however, not only claims to be a product of the supernatural in the form of the miraculous, it claims finality. Hence either its claim of finality is well-grounded or its truthfulness can no longer be maintained. According to the high supernaturalism of Christianity, there is not only the possibility but the actuality of two different kinds or modes of activity in God—one through and concurring with natural causes and one direct and immediate and so independent of natural causes. As basically the product of the latter mode of activity, Christianity claims to be the one God-made religion as over against what may be called the man-made religions. If this claim is well-grounded then, but only then, is its claim to finality valid.

The task we have assumed does not include the attempt to prove either the truthfulness or the finality of Christianity. We have sought, however, to indicate what is meant when we speak of the truthfulness of Christianity and to make clear that the question of the finality of Christianity is bound up with the question whether Christianity is true both in the sense of "truth of fact" and "truth of idea."

Surely it must be clear to all that the question of the finality of Christianity is not a merely academic question. Rather it is a question of the utmost practical importance. Not only does it have a far-reaching bearing on our estimate of the need of foreign missions, it has a determining influence on our estimate of the value of Christianity itself. Deny its finality and our whole outlook upon the future is transformed. Then we have no assurance that we have a hope that will never put us to shame. Affirm its finality and we can continue to encourage one another to be steadfast, unmoveable, always abounding in the work of the Lord, forasmuch as we know that our labor is not in vain in the Lord (I Cor. 15:58). Deny its finality and we can have no assurance that Christianity will not one day become that saddest of all things—a dead religion. But affirm it, and we can face the future confident that at the end of the years all that is opposed to Christ will have been brought into subjection and that the time is coming when in a kingdom that shall know no end, a great multitude, which no man can number, "out of every nation and all tribes and peoples and tongues," will be gathered before the Lamb upon His throne and join in the great jubilation: "Unto Him that loves us, and washed us from our sins by His blood; and He made us to be a kingdom, to be priests unto His God and Father; to Him be the glory and the dominion for ever and ever. Amen."

INDEX

INDEX